A History

of the

Diocese

of

Lafayette-in-Indiana

By Reverend Anthony Prosen, S.T.L., Ph. D.

Author
Reverend Anthony Prosen, S.T.L., Ph. D.

Assisted by
Msgr. Robert L. Sell III, Vicar General
Thomas Russell, Head, Pastoral Office for Planning and Communications

Consultants:
Dr. Elizabeth Glenn, Chapter One.
Mike Witka, Our Lady of Grace, Noblesville
Father Melvin Bennett, St. Anthony, Dehners Corner
Dolores Rench, St. Lawrence, Muncie
Father Donald Gross, Sacred Heart, Fowler, and St. Mary, Dunnington
Joseph Abel, St. Mary, Anderson
Father David Newton, Holy Family, Gas City
Carmen Doyle, St. Mary, Muncie
Rick Root, St. Mary, Union City
Helen Davies and Sheryl Thurston, St. Joseph, Winchester
Dick Pierce and Jan Scarcelli, Blessed Sacrament, West Lafayette
Richard Copeland, All Saints, Logansport
Dr. James Bayley, Cathedral of St. Mary of the Immaculate Conception, Lafayette
Janice Hackbush, archivist, Diocese of Fort Wayne-South Bend
Dr. Kevin Cawley, archivist, University of Notre Dame
And all general parish contributors

Readers
Dr. James Davidson
Dr. Anne D. Roat

Staff
Laurie Cullen

Editor
Loretta Pastva, SND

Photography
John Glover

Publisher
Éditions du Signe • B.P. 94
67038 Strasbourg cedex 2 • France
Tél: (++33) 3 88 78 91 91
Fax: (++33) 3 88 78 91 99
Email: info@editionsdusigne.fr

Publishing Director
Christian Riehl

Director of Publication
Joëlle Bernhard

Publishing Assistant
Audrey Gilger

Design and Layout
Daniel Muller - M@W

Photoengraving
Atelier du Signe - 106927

ISBN-10: 2-7468-1682-2
ISBN-13: 978-2-7468-1682-4

Printed in China

PRAISED BE JESUS CHRIST!
(NOW AND FOREVER)

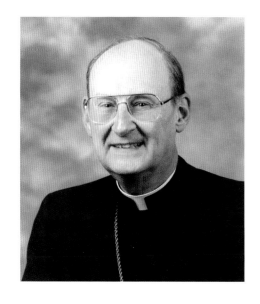

SHORTLY AFTER OCTOBER 21, 1944, while the world bled through the horror of WWII, Catholics living in the 24 counties of North Central Indiana learned that they belonged to a new Diocese. At the direction of Pope Pius XII it would be known as the Diocese of Lafayette-in-Indiana. The 9,832 square miles so named had already been a part of five different Church jurisdictions: Quebec, Baltimore, Bardstown (Kentucky), Vincennes and Fort Wayne.

In the history of the Diocese of Lafayette-in-Indiana it is hoped the reader will capture an idea of how our Local Church developed over 300 years of colonial and American history to its 60th anniversary.

Éditions du Signe editors acknowledge the efforts of Father Anthony Prosen, the primary writer; Monsignor Robert L. Sell, III, Vicar General; Thomas Russell, head of the Pastoral Office for Planning and Communications, and his staff, especially Laurie Cullen. They are grateful to its critical readers Dr. James Davidson and Dr. Anne Roat. They acknowledge parish contributors. I too am most grateful to these contributors and praise God for the people whose lives wrote the history of our Church, and continue to do so.

Not only does this history outline how our Diocese came to be and how it has developed, but also provides a framework to recall much more than it tells. It hands on a challenge to its readers to accomplish even greater things in service to the Gospel of Jesus Christ here in the Diocese of Lafayette-in-Indiana.

May the blessings of the past inspire us to have confidence that the Risen Lord will be present to us in our future as we strive to make him better known and loved.

Assuring you and your families of my prayers and best wishes, I remain

Sincerely yours in Christ,

William L. Higi
Bishop of Lafayette-in-Indiana

PRAISED BE JESUS CHRIST

Table of Contents

A HISTORY OF THE DIOCESE OF LAFAYETTE-IN-INDIANA

PARISHES

Part One

A History

of the

Diocese

of

Lafayette-in-Indiana

1844 map of U.S. Dioceses

Chapter 1
MISSIONARY TIMES

THE Diocese of Lafayette-in-Indiana comprises 24 of Indiana's 92 counties; namely, Benton, Blackford, Boone, Carroll, Cass, Clinton, Delaware, Fountain, Fulton, Grant, Hamilton, Howard, Jasper, Jay, Madison, Miami, Montgomery, Newton, Pulaski, Randolph, Tippecanoe, Tipton, Warren and White counties. Pope Pius XII established this diocese on October 21, 1944, and named it "Lafayette-in-Indiana" to distinguish it from the Diocese of Lafayette, Louisiana, which had already been established since 1918.

The Cathedral of St. Mary of the Immaculate Conception in Lafayette is the cathedral church for the diocese. (A "cathedral" is the central church of a diocese, where the bishop's chair -- or "cathedra"-- sits, symbolizing his authority.) The church that became the diocesan cathedral developed from Lafayette's SS. Mary and Martha Church, 1844-1866. St. Mary's principal benefactor at its 1866 completion was a Potawatomi descendant of French fur traders at nearby Fort Ouiatanon, William Burnett Davis.

Indiana's French colonization heritage is important in diocesan history. British colonies occupied the eastern seaboard of the United States, while the land of this future diocese was in New France, which extended from Quebec to New Orleans west of the Allegheny Mountains to the northern Pacific Ocean. Indiana was in an area called the Illinois Country. Unlike British colonists, French colonists were neither religious nor political dissenters, nor prisoners seeking respite in the colonies. On the contrary, French colonists had to be certified as religiously and politically capable and willing to present France's mission among the native inhabitants with whom they were to engage in commerce. The British discriminated against the natives as savages, but the French policy had no such prejudice. The French colonists' mission to evangelize the inhabitants led many to intermarry without discrimination.

DIOCESE OF QUEBEC

FRENCH Catholic colonists were supervised initially by the archdioceses of Rouen and Rennes, from which many came. Because in 1658 the Catholic religion was flourishing at Quebec, Pope Innocent X appointed Blessed

◆ *Old Cathedral in Vincennes*

Francois Xavier de Montmorenci Laval as his apostolic vicar to oversee the Catholic churches. In 1674, Pope Clement IX named Bishop Laval the first bishop of the Diocese of Quebec. From Notre Dame de Quebec Cathedral, Bishop Laval supervised all of New France. He designated missionary priests to be his vicars general in different places. In the Illinois Country, he gave this assignment to the priests of the Society of Jesus. The dividing line between New France's provinces of Quebec and New Orleans was at Terre Haute, which the British later called "the Highland."

Father Pierre Gibault, a priest of the Quebec diocese, was its last vicar general in the Illinois Country. Father Gibault's

Sainte Anne de Detroit
est. 1711, completed 1828, razed 1886
rebuilt at Nineteenth and Howard Streets
1886

◆ Ste. Anne Church, Detroit

statue outside the Old Cathedral in Vincennes recognizes him as "the patriot priest." This recalls that during the American Revolution, American colonists were concerned that the British might attack them from the West. In 1763 the British had taken New France from the French and the Illinois County became known as the Northwest Territory of Canada. George Rogers Clark's Virginia militia went West to secure the already existing French posts. When he came to Vincennes in 1787, Father Gibault discussed with Clark the American intention to guarantee religious freedom in its Constitution. Besides the French revulsion for the British, the fact that the Church of England is the state-established Church in Great Britain and its colonies was a religious dilemma. Clark agreed to Father Gibault's suggestion to hold a two-day parish consultation. The parishioners met in St. Francis Xavier Church and gave their assent to become Americans. Local inhabitants were astounded when the people came out of the church and raised a handmade American flag, meaning the whole area was now Virginia's territory. The Altar Society ladies, who hastily sewed the flag using red and green Christmas bunting, gave Father Gibault the bill. The British sent General Henry Hamilton to recapture Vincennes while Father Gibault went into exile in Missouri. But General Clark took it back and the Northwest

Territory made it possible for the U.S. Congress to create the Indiana Territory with Vincennes as its capital in 1800.

STE. ANNE, DETROIT PARISHIONERS

OUIATANON was not chosen by chance for the post. Already in 1703 Pierre Roy had married Marguerite Ouabankioue of the Miami at Ouiatanon. Their marriage is recorded at Ste. Anne, Detroit. It is the parish register's second entry after the record of the baptism of the child of Detroit's founder, the Sieur de Cadillac. Their daughter, Marie Louise Roy, educated at Quebec, received a permit on July 4, 1725, to ride in Sieur Aveline's canoe to visit her parents at Ouiatanon. The Roys became the great-grandparents by way of Chief Pacanne of Indiana's famous Chief John Baptist Richardville. (Father Michael Clarke held his funeral in 1841 in what became Fort Wayne's Cathedral Square.) Jean Richard, the post blacksmith and interpreter, also married a Ouiatanon girl and had three children by 1722. In 1852 his granddaughter Angelique married Donatian Richardville at St. Francis Xavier Cathedral, Vincennes.

The first native-born priest from what became Indiana was born at Ouiatanon. On July 22, 1741, Anthony Faucher was born there to Marie Louise Lefebvre and her husband John Baptist Faucher. Baptized on the same day, it was only when the Fox uprising threatened the settlers and his parents were returning to Montreal on July 17, 1748, that they could stop at Ste. Anne, Detroit, for the Ouiatanon baptism to be confirmed. Friar Bonaventure Liénard, Recollect missionary, on page 29 of the register records his parents' names and

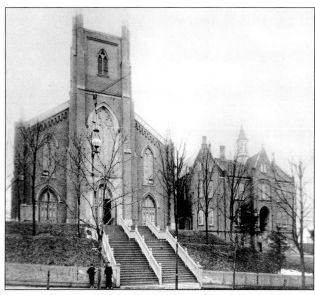

◆ St. Mary's and St. Ignatius Academy, Lafayette

godparents Claude Drouet de Carqueville, Sieur de Richarville [sic] and Mademoiselle Gauché. After Bishop Jean Oliver Briand ordained Anthony a priest on October 30, 1773, Father Faucher served three Quebec area parishes until his death at age 70 on June 1, 1812, at Lachenaie, Quebec. He is buried at St. Henri de Mascouche parish cemetery, Quebec.

Bishop Henri-Marie Pontbriand visited Ste. Anne, Detroit, in 1741. This is as far south as the bishops of Quebec traveled. The official trading posts came to be run by independent families like the Roys, Richardvilles, LaFontaines, Cicots, Gamelins and others who also had Indian names. John Baptist Richardville, for example, used Peshawa (Wildcat); Pierre Moran, Chief Parish or Perig; Charles de Mete, Chief Metea, and so on, depending on the circumstances.

Ouiatanon's settlers were related from the very beginning with fathers and sons, brothers and cousins from Quebec, then through their Miami or Potawatomi wives, and later through their Indiana resident French and Indian descendants. The Chevaliers, Bertrands, and Burnetts ran their posts from St. Joseph, Michigan-Indiana, the Godfroys and Richardvilles, on the Wabash River. Between the American Revolutionary War and the War of 1812, there were many intrigues in the Northwest Territory as Great Britain sought Indian sympathy to regain its lost colonies. Ouiatanon being a popular gathering place was the reason it made the list for the United States Army to burn it down in 1791.

OUIATANON'S TRANSITION

In the many battles waged to secure its territory, the United States rewarded loyal Indians and army veterans with land grants. And so, an unusual development occurred when the United States government was removing Indians from Indiana Territory and state after 1800 and 1816. The government was giving land grants or reserves to Indiana resident French and Indian descendants now considered Americans, while expelling those it considered Indians not yet Americans. Since the American French and Indian descendants' principal proof of identity was their baptismal certificate, preservation of their Catholic religion concerned them, and this affected the Church's history in Indiana.

When General Charles Scott reported on Ouiatanon's destruction in 1791 he wrote from Lexington, Kentucky, that many inhabitants were still French and "lived in a state of civilization." Their books, letters, and other documents made it evident that they depended on Detroit. Scott's troops also burned a large quantity of corn, a variety of household goods, peltry and other articles. The hamlet consisted of 70 houses, "many of them well finished."

The people did not immediately leave the area but withdrew to the countryside. Only when Eastern seaboard Irish and German immigrants, preoccupied with their own ethnic identity, later ignored them did many move to the western United States.

◈ Elaine Barlow's depiction of Fort Ouiatanon in 1752

OUIATANON INHABITANTS SETTLED OUT

BISHOP Simon Bruté's 1835 hand-drawn map shows that he visited Independence, Warren County, passing through Peru, Logansport and Lafayette. At Independence, he stopped to see Zachariah Cicot whose trapper father and Ouiatanon mother had lived and traded at Fort Ouiatanon. Born near Big Spring in 1781, Zachariah was educated at St. Francis Xavier, Vincennes, then returned to manage a trading post. Though the Potawatomi did not like his American allegiance and made his brother George Chief, after the War of 1812 his wise allegiance found him on the winning side.

Having served the American cause, Zachariah received from Indiana Territory's Governor William Henry Harrison a house manufactured in the model of his own Grouseland mansion and shipped from Vincennes up the Wabash River to be assembled as the first house north of Indiana's 1817 boundary. In October 1817, Zachariah married Elizabeth Moran, daughter of the Potawatomi Chief Parish, also known as Pierre Moran. Zachariah laid out Independence on Cicot reserve property that he had to purchase from land granted his son John Baptist. After his death in 1850 he was buried beside his wife Elizabeth in the Independence Cemetery. Warren County's bigoted settlers tore down the "Indian" house and used its wood for plank roads.

On June 17, 1837, Bishop Bruté bought Lot 68 for a church in Independence, but none was ever built. From 1838-1883 Independence and Williamsport continued to be listed in Catholic directories as sites visited by missionary priests from Logansport, Lafayette, Attica and Covington.

BURNETT'S LEGACY

AFTER William Digby laid out Lafayette in 1825 on a land track purchased from Pierre Langlois, whose Ouiatanon relatives had extended their trading to Logansport, William Davis was running a mill and a still at his ferry on the Wabash River near Wildcat Creek. He had married Nancy (Ann) Burnett, one of the many children of the Burnett trading family. They had two sons, Richard and William. Through a series of events, Nancy became sole heir to all the land reserves the government had granted her five brothers and sister. Upon her

◆ George Winter's sketch of Bishop Bruté at Logansport (Courtesy Tippecanoe County Historical Association)

death she willed her estate to her sons. After Richard's untimely death, William Burnett Davis became the sole heir. Known as "Indian Bill" to ignorant contemporaries, Mr. Davis resided at the American Hotel, Lafayette, where he became a friend of Father George Hamilton. Most likely, this friendship developed with the help of Sisters of Providence Mother Cecilia Bailly, herself a descendant of the Ottawa from Michigan. Mother Cecilia was a frequent visitor to her Sisters' school in Lafayette and resided there for a year upon completion of her term as Mother Superior.

At his September 6, 1866, death, "Indian Bill" left his entire estate to the Church for St. Mary's Church and for the support of indigent orphans, naming Father Hamilton his executor. The entire estate was valued at about $75,000 in 19th century money and included the Burnett land reserves. When Father Hamilton was still finalizing the estate in 1870, he advertised more than 3,400 acres. He himself bought four lots from the Bishop of Fort Wayne who held the property's titles. These titles were transferred to the Bishop of Lafayette-in-Indiana in 1944. After Father Hamilton's death on April 6, 1876, the St. Joseph Orphan Asylum and Manual Labor School opened at Lafayette and operated until 1937.

In St. Mary Cemetery, Lafayette, a stone reads: "In memory of William B. Davis, grandson of Cakimi, a Potawatomi woman,

The gravestone reads:
IN MEMORY OF
WILLIAM B. DAVIS
GRANDSON OF
CAKIMI
A POTAWATOMI
WOMAN,
SISTER OF
TOPIMIBE
PRINCIPAL CHIEF
OF THE
POTAWATOMI
TRIBE OF INDIANS
BORN IN
TIPPECANOE CO.
IND. IN 1829
AND DIED
SEPT. 6. 1866
REQUIESCAT
IN PACE

◆ Inscription on Indian Bill gravestone

sister of Tipimibe, Principal Chief of the Potawatomie Tribe of Indians. Born in Tippecanoe County in 1829 and died September 6, 1866. Requiescat in Pace."

ST. ANNE'S COMMEMORATION

WABASH River travelers belonged to Ste. Anne Parish, Detroit, until St. Francis Xavier, Vincennes, gave them another parish church. Priests known to have attended and occasionally resided at Ouiatanon included Jesuit missionary Fathers John Mermet, 1698-1716; Joseph Marest, 1702-1711; Charles Guimoneau, 1722-1725; Pierre DuJaunay, 1738-1765, and Sebastian Louis Meurin, 1764. Between missionary visits, the priest would appoint a literate parishioner to serve as notary for baptisms, marriages and funerals, and to lead prayers in his absence.

People remembered Ste. Anne's by naming many chapels along the rivers in her honor. Among other things she is a patron saint of voyageurs and waterway travelers. When Father Francis Xavier Nigh was evangelizing the upper Tippecanoe River settlements about 1855-1862, he found missions of St. Anne (1851) near Monterey, St. Ann (1852) near Pulaski, both in Pulaski County, and built St. Ann's (about 1858) at Grass Creek, Fulton County. It may not be a coincidence that Father Hamilton built St. Ann's Chapel on Wabash Avenue, Lafayette, in 1870 and named it for "Indian Bill's" mother's patron saint. Holy Cross Brothers ran a boys' school there until it became a parish in 1884. Since February 9, 1933, St. Ann Church and Shrine has enshrined a relic of Good St. Ann from the Shrine of Ste. Anne de Beaupré, Quebec.

◆ *St. Ann Shrine and relic, Lafayette*

DIOCESES OF BALTIMORE AND BARDSTOWN

NINETEEN years after Pope Pius VI created the United States' first Diocese of Baltimore (1789), Pope Pius VII made its Bishop John Carroll archbishop of the Baltimore ecclesiastical province. Thus, in 1808, Archbishop Carroll's province included the suffragan dioceses of New Orleans (1793), Boston, New York, Philadelphia, Pennsylvania; and Bardstown, Kentucky. After arriving in Kentucky in 1811, Bishop Benedict Flaget of the Diocese of Bardstown cared for the Indiana Territory and state (after 1816). Having ordained a friend and classmate of Bishop Flaget, Father Stephen Badin, the United States' first priest in 1793, Bishop Carroll sent him to evangelize Kentucky before the Bardstown diocese was established. Since missionary priests were able to transact property in their own name, a friendly altercation developed when Bishop Flaget arrived and asked Father Badin to transfer property titles to the diocese.

Father Badin took a leave to the Diocese of Orleans, France. When he returned he went to the Diocese of Cincinnati. Bishop John Baptist Purcell sent him to the Potawatomi missions, 1828-1829, at the Michigan-Indiana border. After a year back in Cincinnati, he returned, 1830-1836, and established St. Joseph mission at the south bend

◆ *Father John Bennett's St. Ann mural at St. Joseph, Garrett*

DIOCESE OF VINCENNES

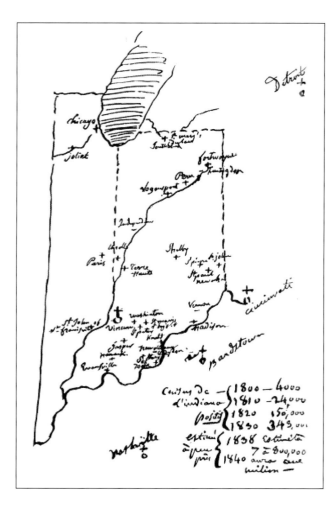

◈ *Map sketched by Bishop Bruté*

UPON recommendation of the Second Provincial Council of Baltimore (1833), Pope Gregory XVI created the Diocese of Vincennes for Indiana and eastern Illinois on May 8, 1834. The Eastern seaboard political and religious community was startled when Archbishop James Whitfield of Baltimore sent the president of Mount St. Mary College, Emmitsburg, Maryland, Father William Simon Gabriel Bruté de Remur as the first bishop of Vincennes. The Eastern seaboard mindset was such that the West was wild. They did not consider that for almost 150 years the Diocese of Quebec had developed a culture among the territory's inhabitants. Its parishioners were accustomed to sending their children to schools at Detroit, Montreal or Quebec. A highly educated priest, Bishop Bruté brought with him an extensive library and immediately pioneered many schools among his flock. While he served as Mount St. Mary's president, he had been spiritual director to St. Elizabeth Ann Seton whose Sisters of Charity had their convent nearby. At her death in 1821, St. Elizabeth Ann willed her Bible to Father Bruté. It can be seen at the Old Cathedral Library, Vincennes.

Bishop Bruté's mission visitation map shows that there had long been sites missionaries stopped at on the Wabash

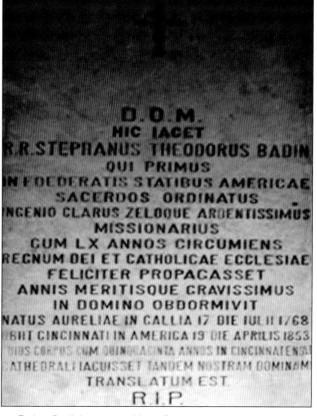

◈ *Father Badin's grave at Notre Dame*

of the St. Joseph River where he built a log chapel while residing with the Potawatomi Chief Pokagon. Father Badin could travel Indiana's first north-south road, which the Potawatomi agreed could be laid out in 1828. This Michigan Road went from Michigan City to Logansport to Indianapolis. In an 1834 letter, Father Badin relates that he took Wabash-Erie Canal trips from Logansport to Peru where he bought two acres for a church in 1831. After he returned to Cincinnati and the Diocese of Bardstown relocated to Louisville in 1841, he transferred his title to a farm on former Potawatomi land that he purchased from the United States government to Father Edward Sorin of the Congregation of the Holy Cross to start the University of Notre Dame.

Bishop Flaget, whom Bishop Carroll had sent as missionary to Vincennes in 1792-1795, visited St. Francis Xavier Church there occasionally during 1814-1818, holding the first confirmation celebration in Indiana there in 1814. St. Francis Xavier's records continue from April 21, 1749.

River, as well as the south bend of the St. Joseph River and upper Tippecanoe River. When Logansport became a land office in 1828 and an annuity distribution center in 1838, it became a mission base, too, as the Wabash-Erie Canal arrived. Many Logansport residents had liaisons between Vincennes, Lafayette, and the Potawatomi on the upper Tippecanoe River. The artist George Winter made a sketch of Bishop Bruté preaching to the Potawatomi near Logansport on their 1838 expulsion from Indiana to Kansas the year before his death in June 1839.

Both Vincennes' Bishops Celestine de la Hailandiere, 1839-1847, and Maurice de St. Palais, 1848-1877, continued visiting their Wabash River missions. Bishop de St. Palais, indeed, had been a missionary to Chicago where he built St. Mary Church, which became the Diocese of Chicago's first cathedral when Illinois was separated from the Diocese of Vincennes in 1843. Father de St. Palais was a missionary at Logansport, 1844-1846. While travel on the Wabash-Erie Canal began in 1832 from Toledo, Ohio, to Terre Haute, the Vincennes' bishops found that Catholics immigrating from Ireland's northern counties to dig canal locks and towpaths were amalgamating with the American French and Indian Catholics already established in Indiana. Bishop Bruté's immediate successor in 1839 was permitted to establish his residence at Lafayette, Vincennes, Madison or Indianapolis. He chose to remain at Vincennes.

◈ *Bishop Bruté*

EDUCATION AND WORKS OF CHARITY

AFTER Bishop Bruté's arrival, Indiana's Catholics promoted education and works of charity. From 1836, the Sisters of Charity of Nazareth, Kentucky, were running St. Clare's Convent and Female Academy, Vincennes, to provide religious education for the Wabash River inhabitants' daughters. The next year this became known as the Academy of the Sisters of Charity of Vincennes. In 1839, St. Elizabeth Ann Seton's Sisters of Charity from Emmitsburg, Maryland, replaced it with St. Mary's Female Academy.

In 1841 Blessed Mother Theodore Guerin announced that her Sisters of Providence, newly arrived in Indiana, were opening St. Mary of the Woods School near Terre Haute.

◈ *St. Elizabeth Ann Seton (Image courtesy Catholic News Service)*

At Lafayette, St. Mary of the Woods alumnae taught in a school behind SS. Mary and Martha Church. Here the Sisters of Providence came to open St. Mary's Female Academy in 1858 prior to their 1861 acquisition of property for St. Ignatius Academy. Catholic Sisters at this time taught only girls and young women. By 1853, the Sisters of Providence had also begun a school in Fort Wayne and altogether had seven schools in Indiana.

Bishop Bruté opened a Catholic college at Vincennes in 1837. He secured the Society of the Sacred Hearts of Jesus and Mary (Eudists) to run a theological seminary there, too. After his death in 1839, the college became known as St. Gabriel College.

In 1841, the Brothers of St. Joseph announced the opening of a novitiate at St. Peter's near Washington in Daviess County. By 1844, Father Edward Sorin made a School for Young Men at St. Peter's. The Brothers of St. Joseph then became associated with the Congregation of the Holy Cross of

◆ *Bishop de St. Palais*

English and Irish priests were trained at French seminaries in Normandy and Brittany. In 1841, Father Michael Clarke was ordained at Vincennes Cathedral. Bishop de la Hailandiere sent him to Fort Wayne, 1841-1842; Peru, 1842; and finally, after the Vicar General of Vincennes, Father Simon Lalumiere, had visited Lafayette in 1843, appointed him the pastor of Lafayette. The following year SS. Mary and Martha Church – "the handsomest church edifice in Indiana, and regarded as superior to all in northern Indiana"– was built. Father Clarke's parish extended through Tippecanoe, Fountain, Warren, Montgomery, Madison, Benton, Putnam, Carroll and White counties. He also ministered to Catholics along the old Strawtown Trail (roughly today's State Road 32), Indiana's first west-east route. He traveled through Boone, Hamilton, Madison, Delaware and Randolph counties. He became charmed with the Randolph County seat, Winchester, one of Indiana's oldest (1818) counties, and intended to reside there; however, he remained at Lafayette until 1857.

Father Daniel Molony, from St. John Church, Indianapolis, 1853-1855, followed Father Clarke at

which Father Sorin was the superior. This was shortly after Father Sorin announced the foundation of the University of Notre Dame du Lac by the priests of the Holy Cross, St. Joseph College by the Brothers of the Holy Cross, and St. Mary Academy by the Sisters of the Holy Cross, all in St. Joseph County. (This was on the land Father Badin had given with the approval of the Bishop of Vincennes.) The priests and Brothers moved there, but the Sisters' novitiate was located at Berrien, Michigan.

Free schools for orphans were provided, too. From 1838 the Sisters of Charity ran a Free School for girls next to their Academy, and the diocese provided a Male Free School taught by the Brothers of St. Joseph at Vincennes. At Vincennes, Bishop de St. Palais had the Sisters of Providence open St. Mary Female Asylum for orphans in 1849, and in 1850, after the Brothers left for Notre Dame, he persuaded them to take charge of St. Vincent Male Orphan Asylum for children. By 1853, the Sisters of the Third Order of St. Francis had arrived at Oldenburg and opened their Immaculate Conception Academy.

MISSION EXPANSION FROM THE WABASH

FRENCH missionaries providentially were able to recruit English-speaking priests from France because when the English Reformation closed seminaries in Ireland,

◆ *Blessed Mother Theodore Guerin (Image courtesy Sisters of Providence)*

Ss. Mary and Martha Church prior to being razed, 1953

GERMANS ARRIVE

WHEN the 1848 Liberal Revolution in Germany failed, the first waves of German immigrants arrived in the Midwest. Unlike earlier migrants and the 1850 Potato Famine immigrants from Ireland who had worked on railroads, these were farmers, skilled tradesmen and business entrepreneurs. Bankrupt by the Canal failure in 1837, Indiana rewrote its Constitution in 1851 to prohibit the state from ever again going into debt. This combination welcomed enterprising immigrants on the eve of the War Between the States. They strengthened the North's economic ideas and provided a wedge for the elimination of the South's idea of a slave labor force. At this time there was slavery in Indiana, as well.

Lafayette and on this Trail. He ministered to missions at Frankfort, Sheridan, Lebanon, Pendleton, Anderson, Muncie, Winchester and Union City, prior to his departure for the Diocese of Dubuque in 1860. Priests from Indianapolis, Logansport, Peru and even Shelbyville also visited Strawtown and Boxley, Hamilton County, and Pendleton, Madison County, during this time.

This area covers the Diocese of Lafayette-in-Indiana's history. Counties north of the Wabash River were being created only after the Potawatomi 1832 land session, and the Miami Reserves were retained until 1839. So Tippecanoe (1829), Fountain (1825), Carroll (1828), Cass (1829), Delaware (1827), Grant (1831), Hamilton (1823), Madison (1823), Miami (1828), Montgomery (1828), Clinton (1830), Boone (1830), Warren (1827) and Randolph (1818) counties were on their way to development before counties north of the Wabash River existed. Other than Wabash River counties, only LaPorte, St. Joseph, Porter and LaGrange counties lined Indiana's northern border.

The other half of the present diocese's counties: Benton (1840/1843); Blackford (1838), Fulton (1836), Jasper (1838), Jay (1836), Newton (1838/1859), Pulaski (1840), White (1835), Howard (1844/1859) and Tipton (1844) were just begun. The disposition of the Miami Reserves affected some of them. Were one to impose the crescent pattern of today's I-65, I-465, I-69 from Lafayette to Carmel to Muncie, this would be the described area. The original Lafayette parish of SS. Mary and Martha Church virtually encompassed the present diocese to which this history is confined.

To Lafayette, Bishop de St. Palais sent Father William Doyle, a native of Pennsylvania Dutch country near Pittsburgh who had been reared in Logansport, to meet with SS. Mary and Martha's burgeoning congregation on December 25, 1853, to organize from it the new St. Boniface Church. Although there would be many ethnic groups composing the diocese's parishes in its history, this was the only one actually established for an ethnic group.

To provide for the German influx, Bishop de St. Palais allowed his Vicar General, Father Joseph Kundek of Jasper, to invite the monks of the Order of St. Benedict from Einsiedeln, Switzerland, to found St. Meinrad Abbey in Spencer County in 1853. When the Benedictines arrived in Vincennes, Bishop de St. Palais' cordial greetings included him saying, "I indeed foresee that this diocese will soon have to be divided, and I should very much like to see that a place near the episcopal city would be to your liking.... "

In 1850 the Diocese of Vincennes had come into the province of the Archdiocese of Cincinnati. Already at the First Plenary Council of Baltimore (1852), the American bishops had recommended to Blessed Pius IX that northern Indiana receive a bishop. On September 22, 1857, Blessed Pius IX acceded and created the Diocese of Fort Wayne out of the northern half of the Diocese of Vincennes from Fountain, Montgomery, Boone, Hamilton, Madison, Delaware and Randolph counties to the Indiana-Michigan border. This coincided with the colonization of northern Indiana, which brings a new chapter to the development of the Diocese of Lafayette-in-Indiana's history.

New France protested to Pope Clement X his synodal decree to excommunicate any businessman trafficking in liquor. His successor, Bishop Jean Baptiste de la Croix Chevriere de St. Valier, held four synods to stimulate the missions in the Mississippi Valley between 1688-1727.

To regulate Church practice in the United States there had been seven Baltimore provincial councils between 1829-1849. In 1852, 1866, and 1884, there were three plenary councils dealing with all matters of Church life. From 1865-89, there would also be five Provincial Councils of Cincinnati. Thus the missionary Church in the United States was becoming well organized.

In the Diocese of Vincennes in 1844, Bishop Hailandiere held a synod to attempt to implement Church regulations such as requiring altar societies to guarantee altar maintenance for any church reserving the Blessed Sacrament. Men of a parish were expected to care for the building and grounds. No new church henceforth could be built without written permission of the bishop. Particularly during northern Indiana's colonization, this latter rule was ignored. Bishop Hailandiere became very unpopular and resigned in 1847. His successor, Bishop de St. Palais, held no synods. Bishop Luers held policy-making synods with clergy when they made biennial retreats at Notre Dame. Besides coping with the influence of the War Between the States, 1861-1865, Bishop Luers had his hands full organizing the Church in northern Indiana.

◆ *Bishop Luers*

THE ARRIVAL OF BISHOP LUERS

WHAT did Bishop Luers find in the 24 counties that are now the Diocese of Lafayette-in-Indiana? From churches on the Wabash River priests had spread north and south to meet the colonizing Catholics. From 1857-1903, all churches were considered missions. The United States was in the jurisdiction of the Roman Congregation for the Propagation of the Faith. Its principal support came from the French-founded Society for the Propagation of the Faith, the Austrian Leopoldine Society and the Bavarian Ludwig Society.

Father Daniel Molony was at SS. Mary and Martha Church, and Father Joseph Stephan at St. Boniface Church, Lafayette. Father Molony was caring for missions at Frankfort, Lebanon, Oxford and Rock Creek Township (Carroll County). Father Stephan took care of missions at Delphi, Francesville, Medaryville, Monticello, Reynolds, Rensselaer and Sugar Creek in Madison Township (Carroll County). Father Stephan had a cottage at San Pierre, Starke

County, out of which he did extensive evangelization wherever a railroad took him. He even directed a colonization society that settled German immigrants in parishes. He also became a military chaplain during the War Between the States.

At Lafayette, Father George Hamilton succeeded Father Molony's successor, Father Edmund Burke Kilroy, who also became a military chaplain in 1863. Father Hamilton attended missions at Reynolds, Frankfort, Oxford, Lebanon, Brookston, Buck Creek, Clarks Hill and Colfax. He built and dedicated Logansport's St. Vincent de Paul Church in 1863. Near the Sisters of Providence's St. Ignatius Academy on Seminary Hill, Lafayette, where Father Kilroy began its foundation, he finished building the Church of St. Mary of the Immaculate Conception in 1866. It was paid for principally from the William Burnett Davis estate. "Indian Bill" also willed his real estate to the Church for the care of orphans, which enabled the 1876 opening of St. Joseph Orphan Asylum and Manual Labor School, Lafayette. At "Indian Bill's" 1866 death, Father Hamilton had intended to bury the benefactor in the vault next to his own beneath St. Mary's. The vault is there, but "Indian Bill" lies buried in St. Mary Cemetery, Lafayette. In 1867, Father Hamilton

Kokomo, Kniman, Tipton, Bunker Hill, Rochester, Fairmount, Arcadia, Marion, Strawtown, Galveston, Royal Centre and Wabash.

Father William Doyle, whom Father Augustus Martin had sent from Logansport to study for the priesthood at Vincennes, came to St. Vincent de Paul from St. Boniface, Lafayette, in 1855. From Lagro, Father John Ryan visited Jonesboro and Marion. In the upper Tippecanoe River area of Pulaski County, Father Francis Xavier Nigh, living with a private family, was visiting many missions, especially St. Anne's with its upper and lower settlement on either side of the river. Two parishioners at Monterey deeded four acres to Bishop de St. Palais in 1851.

At Mary's Home, Jay County, a Convent of Sisters of the Precious Blood with Father Sebastian Gander as chaplain was discovered. At Lafayette, the Sisters of Providence from St. Mary of the Woods had opened St. Mary Female Institute on Sixth Street behind SS. Mary and Martha Church.

BISHOP LUERS LINGERED AT LAFAYETTE

BISHOP Luers delayed his arrival in Fort Wayne with a year's stay in Lafayette. Father Daniel Molony hosted him at SS. Mary and Martha's. There he ordained Father Martin Scherer to the priesthood on October 24, 1858. This was the first ordination in northern Indiana. Father Scherer celebrated his first Mass of Thanksgiving at St. Boniface Church on October 31 and was sent to serve the German congregation at the LaPorte Church of the Nativity of the Blessed Virgin Mary. In 1860 he was made pastor of the separate parish of St. Joseph there. Later he transferred to the Archdiocese of St. Louis where he died.

Since his cathedral city was not yet firmly set, Bishop Luers would have made his cathedral in Lafayette, but by one vote the city council refused him the property he intended for the site. He then proceeded to Fort Wayne where he found a dilapidated frame Church of St. Augustine that became his first cathedral, and Mary the Mother of God Church a few blocks away serving a German congregation.

◆ *Father Hamilton burial site*

◆ *Father George Hamilton*

instituted St. Ann's Chapel on Wabash Avenue for railroad travelers near the Holy Cross Brothers' Boys School.

From Crawfordsville, Father Edward O'Flaherty visited Attica, Covington and State Line City (Warren County). From Anderson, Father Michael Clarke visited Muncie, Noblesville, Winchester and Union City. From Logansport, Fathers Charles Zucker and George Hamilton visited Cicero, Kokomo, Peru, Pleasant Grove (Kewanna, Fulton County), Pulaski and Winamac. Bishop Bruté had been to Logansport in 1838 to dedicate the stone church of St. Vincent de Paul to replace an 1835 log mission for canal workers. From Logansport, Father Clarke also visited Peru and Lafayette until 1844. When Father Bernard Kroeger was at Logansport in 1863 he cared for missions at Kewanna, Harrison and Pulaski; then at Peru, he attended missions at Lagro,

REV. G. A. HAMILTON

WHOSE REMAINS ARE ENTOMBED BENEATH THIS SLAB Was born in Marion Co. Ky. April 1819 AND DIED IN Lafayette April 8, 1875. This magnificent Structure as Well as Many others scattered throughout the diocese of Fort Wayne And the neighboring diocese of Chicago are silent witnesses to his zeal and efficiency in the cause of religion.

"*Requiescat in pace.*"

MISSION CHURCHES MULTIPLY

WHEREAS people used to glide along the Wabash and other rivers like superhighways, new towns along railroad tracks made populations stable. While the agrarian economy found the railroads convenient to transport produce, church attendance was inhibited because there were few, if any, roads. Many churches built in this period literally had the railroad at their front doors or were near the tracks, and while parishioners living out in the townships could get to their grain elevator along the tracks, many had no easy way of getting to town.

People subsisting in the agrarian economy relied on large families and their farm produce. At the arrival of the newcomers, Indiana had been a grand forest of trees. As the state's Great Seal illustrates, early settlers believed it was progress to fell the trees to turn Indiana into farmland. Many trees provided wood for building a wide variety of things, including wooden countryside churches.

Many wooden churches for parishioners' convenience sprang up in the countryside. Bishop Herman Alerding's 1907 history of this period often records these as parishes. In fact, they were mission chapels to which the pastor rode a buggy or took the train monthly, bimonthly, quarterly or annually for people who could not get to the main church. Bishop Alerding acknowledges that most of these churches were for more or less a dozen households. These small chapels were a reasonable solution in one sense, because Victorian-era people wore their Sunday best to Mass. They could neither be expected to hike miles through the woods, down a dirt road, nor to wade a creek or river and appear ready for Mass. Nor could they bring along their carry-in dish for the post-Mass dinner in such conditions.

Here is a summary of former churches, some of which became parishes, while others supplemented the parish church. Most were simply missions closed once their purpose was served. The parish sections of this history include even more former churches that were part of the established parish's own history.

COUNTRYSIDE CHURCHES

IN Indian Creek Township, Pulaski County, from 1852 St. Ann's had two churches on either side of the river. One became St. Francis; the other, Assumption of the Blessed Virgin Mary. When a bridge was built across the Tippecanoe River and roads put in, they were consolidated in 1900 into St. Joseph Church, Pulaski.

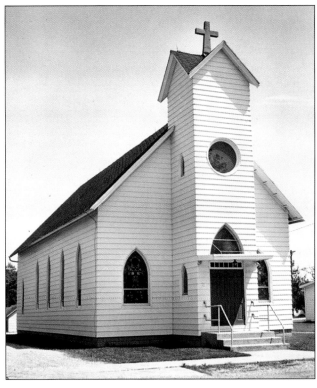

Church of St. Elizabeth, Lucerne, 1905-2001

From 1881-1900 in Pulaski County, Annunciation of the Blessed Virgin Mary, Jefferson Township, had 31 people. According to Fort Wayne directories, it was a mission of Winamac, but Bishop Alerding's 1907 history does not mention it.

At Jay County, people were attending Mass at the Mary's Home Convent until the Sisters of the Precious Blood urged them to build a log church a mile down the road in 1861. The convent chaplains served as its pastors until in 1899 a rectory was built at its 1885 brick Holy Trinity Church. When the rectory became available, the Irish Settlement priest also moved into it. He cared for the Presentation of the Blessed Virgin Mary mission, Adams County, where the Precious Blood Missionaries built a frame church in 1883, replacing it after it burned down in 1885 with a brick church.

At Hamilton County, Busher's Settlement built St. Mary Church, Boxley, and Mullen Settlement built St. John Church, Arcadia, in 1863. These were consolidated into Sacred Heart of Jesus Church, Cicero, in 1901. Cicero itself was a mission of Frankfort, and then of Tipton until 1978 when it became a parish.

At Frushour Settlement, Harrison Township, Cass County, St. Elizabeth Church was built in 1868, and moved into the town of Lucerne in 1905 into the former Evangelical Association church. Its pews and windows were from the brick 1902 Immaculate Conception Church,

Woodville, Carroll County, a mission of Logansport. St. Elizabeth had two resident pastors, 1868-1871, and then became a mission of Kewanna until two more resident pastors, 1953-1964, when it became a mission of Lafayette and Logansport, closing in 2001.

At Grass Creek, Fulton County, St. Ann Church was built for 15 households in 1858 until in 1920 it increased its congregation and moved into the town of Pleasant Grove, later named Kewanna, where a brick St. Ann Church was built for the parish.

In 1873, St. Bridget at the Ditch, Benton County, was built for a dozen households; by 1896, 43 households built a brick church there. After the site was named Barrydale in 1902, its Otterbein mission of St. Charles was erected. In 1931, Barrydale became a mission of the Otterbein church, and after a fire irreparably damaged it, closed in 1991.

From 1879-1905, St. Mary the Virgin Church, Monticello, White County, was attended by the Franciscan Friars, then a mission of the parishes at Reynolds and Remington until its closing.

At Benton County, St. Michael, Talbot, mission from Oxford was attempted in 1874. Then St. Columbkille mission in Hickory Grove Township was built in 1876. When an addition was made in 1877, it was named Holy Trinity and, being without a site name, the missionary called it after himself, Langton. It used the Ambia post office. In 1882, Holy Trinity became a parish; in 1888, the site was civilly named Dunnington. When the second parish church was built in 1893, it was called Nativity of the Blessed Virgin Mary. Finally, in 1952, its third parish church was built and called St. Mary.

ONE COUNTRYSIDE CHURCH'S STORY

ST. Anthony's in Benton County has been documented by Anthony Dehner's own manuscript preserved by Genevieve Dehner Bates and augmented by Elmer Barce's notes. Initially Father Joseph Stephan came from the Rensselaer Indian School between 1863-1869 to hold monthly Mass, using a piano top as an altar, at the Dehner farmhouse until the congregation grew to 19 households. On horseback, Anthony Dehner's son Joseph let neighbors know the Mass time. In 1870, the people hauled materials from Kentland and constructed a wooden, 240-seating capacity 54 x 60-foot church building with a front steeple. About 1880, a bell was installed to replace the Dehner's dinner bell. In 1876, across the road from the 10 acres of cemetery and church, Bernard Quante provided five acres for a priest's house.

By now, Father Anthony Messman from Kentland had been caring for St. Anthony's, but from 1876-1903 the church had resident pastors. In 1903, its priests took up residence in Goodland from where they also served Morocco. Father Francis Koch was sent from Hammond to St. Anthony's in 1903. After Father Bruno Soengen's time, the community was absorbed into SS. Peter and Paul, Goodland, and by 1917 into St. John the Baptist, Earl Park. The building was razed during the 1930s. Its bell was given to St. Jude Church, Fort Wayne. Its statues of the Virgin Mary and Sacred Heart of Jesus have been given to the Cathedral of St. Mary of the Immaculate Conception, Lafayette, for its sacristy and reconciliation room.

◆ St. Anthony, Dehner's Corner

◆ Msgr. Joseph Stephan

In 1870, a memorable Fourth of July picnic was held under the 25-plus tall walnut trees shading a long table in the grove near the Dehner settlement. As a band from Oxford played, Anthony Dehner numbered a thousand people there. Also memorable was the solemn First Communion held on April 30, 1871. Caroline Hasser of Richland Township, Benton County, has kept a 65-year-old card listing the 12 first communicants. From this little congregation, John and Caroline Hasser's daughters, Mary and Minnie, became Sisters Philothea and Alvera, respectively, of the Sisters of St. Francis Seraph of Perpetual Adoration, Lafayette, and their son, Father George Hasser. Father Hasser in 1915 was pastor of St. Mary Mother of God Church, Fort Wayne.

RAILROAD CHURCHES

A T Clarks Hill, Tippecanoe County, St. Rose of Lima was built for 10 households in 1867 and attended monthly by priests taking the train from St. Mary, Lafayette, then the Franciscan Friars from Lafayette, and finally from Lebanon.

At Colfax, Clinton County, St. George was built in 1867 for seven households also cared for by priests from St. Mary,

Lafayette, then the Franciscan Friars, and finally from Lebanon. With St. Rose, it closed by 1932.

A railroad worker church of St. Joseph, called St. Patrick, was built at Marshfield, Warren County, in 1870. Priests and Franciscan Friars from Lafayette attended it from Lafayette until the late 19th century. Missionaries also took the train to visit Catholics in West Lebanon and State Line, Warren County.

Likewise at Coal Creek, Fountain County, an 1875 mission of St. Patrick was built and occasionally visited by priests from Covington until the early 20th century.

At Bunker Hill, Miami County, St. Michael mission was a remodeled shoemaker shop, 1879-1910, for 10, then four, households. Priests rode the train there from Peru, then Kokomo and Marion four or five times a year.

At Veedersburg, Fountain County, St. Mary was built for 11 households from 1897-1946. It was a mission of Covington. Not only did the railroad connect Veedersburg and Covington, but eventually Highway 136 did, and Highway 41 connected it to Attica.

GAS BOOM ERA CHURCHES

I N Delaware County, from 1895-1949, St. Anthony, Albany, was built for 10 households on a site donated by the Cincinnati Syndicate Land Company. It was a mission of Dunkirk until people could take the Interurban to St. Mary Church.

In Jay County, from 1898-1949, St. Patrick, Redkey, was built for five to 10 households as a mission of Dunkirk.

At Fairmount, Grant County, St. Cecilia, 1900-1950, was built and had a pastor, 1900-1907, until its congregation faded with the Gas Boom. It was a mission of Anderson St. John Hospital chaplain until its closing.

At Matthews, Grant County, St. Cecilia's pastor rented the local hall for three households, 1902-07. Matthews was being laid out in the pattern of Washington, D.C., completing only part of Massachusetts Avenue before the Gas Boom deflated its aspirations. It was a bimonthly mission of Fairmount and Anderson.

At Hamilton County, though missionaries had visited Noblesville Catholics since 1839, St. Vincent de Paul Church was built there, 1899-1904, but it closed and was sold when the Gas Boom population moved. Its parishioners took the Interurban to Cicero.

the United States and President Grant pardoned them for violating the federal Constitution forbidding private citizens from conducting foreign invasions. In 1870, Blessed Pius IX persuaded the Archbishop of Armagh to condemn this movement in all its forms. Bishop Luers sent Father McMahon to St. Joseph, Reynolds, where he died on May 28, 1872, and was buried in Lafayette.

EAST CENTRAL INDIANA DEVELOPS

WHILE railroads already had transformed most of the diocese's towns by 1890, the discovery of natural gas in east central Indiana developed its least colonized areas. In 1890, the 63-year-old Bishop Dwenger had gone to New Mexico for rehabilitation of a heart condition; after his return he was confined with his lingering illness until his death on January 23, 1893, at Fort Wayne. His successor, Bishop Joseph Rademacher of Nashville, Tennessee, sent Father Charles Dhe to organize missions in Blackford and Jay counties. Father Dhe built churches at Montpelier, Hartford City, Blackford County; Dunkirk and Redkey, Jay County; and Albany, Delaware County, responding to population growth resulting from the area's natural gas discovery. When the Gas Boom economy collapsed in 1906, its complementary industries like glass manufacturing remained. Father Dhe was sent to Besancon near Fort Wayne for a year and was replaced with Father John Noll before Father Dhe's re-assignment to Sacred Heart of Jesus, Fowler.

Bishop Rademacher dedicated St. Genevieve Church, Gas City (as Harrisburg was renamed), in 1893; St. John the Evangelist, Hartford City, 1894; St. Mary, Dunkirk, 1896; and St. Mary, Alexandria, 1896. In 1896, he also dedicated St. Lawrence, Lafayette.

Bishop Rademacher had been born in Westphalia, Michigan, on December 3, 1840, and was ordained a priest by Bishop Luers in 1863. Among his assignments he served as missionary to Attica where he named the church St. Francis Xavier for the patron of his birth date. He served at Columbia City and Fort Wayne Mary the Mother of God Church before coming to St. Mary, Lafayette, 1880-1883. In 1883, he was made fourth Bishop of Nashville before his transfer to Fort Wayne in 1893. The diocese welcomed him with great enthusiasm. Bishop John Foley of Detroit preached on "the great joy of the clergy and laity" in this historic connection between Detroit and Fort Wayne. When a stroke deteriorated his physical condition in 1899, the Vicar General Father John Henry Guendling, who had come from St. Charles Borromeo, Peru, administered the diocese until Bishop Rademacher died at age 59 on January 12, 1900.

◆ *Bishop Joseph Rademacher*

MISSION DAYS END

AS the 19th century closed, Indiana was 80 percent German in population. The state legislature was considering making German the state's official language. The diocese had been occupied serving orphans and widows left from the War Between the States, inviting religious congregations to open hospitals and promoting parochial schools. Industrialization not only changed the state's rural economic base, but places along railroad lines were also able to build substantial churches.

The dawn of the 20th century brought even more industrialization to the diocese's northwest section when the city of Gary was created. Indeed, the extensive development of Fort Wayne as Indiana's second largest city, the growth of South Bend and the introduction of Interurban train travel and automobiles brought about church transitions that gave northern Indiana its own identity. The Lafayette and Logansport conferences were able to develop more unity in practice and education.

To crown northern Indiana's growth at this point, Pope Leo XIII named the 55-year-old Father Herman Alerding, a priest of the Diocese of Vincennes long before that diocese was renamed Indianapolis in 1898, the fourth Bishop of Fort Wayne on August 30, 1900. It was new leadership in a new century.

◆ *Logansport Deanery clergy, 1940*

Academy, 1874-1898. The closing date for many of the high schools reflected effects of the Great Depression of 1929.

Bishop Dwenger persuaded the Missionaries of the Precious Blood to open Saint Joseph's College, Rensselaer, in 1891. This was after the Orphan Asylum moved the boys to Lafayette and the girls to Fort Wayne (1887) and the Indian Normal School had closed (1896). The Sisters of St. Francis Seraph of Perpetual Adoration ran St. Francis Normal School and College, Lafayette, 1876-1944.

BISHOP ALERDING FACES GREATER THINGS

THE synod summoned by Bishop Alerding in 1903 created the Muncie Deanery consisting of parishes in Delaware, Blackford, Grant, Hamilton, Jay, Madison, Randolph and Tipton counties. He explained that former conferences would be called deaneries and follow county lines. The Lafayette Deanery was defined as Tippecanoe, Benton, Boone, Clinton, Fountain, Montgomery and Warren counties. The Logansport Deanery was to include Cass, Carroll, Fulton, Howard, Jasper, Miami, Newton, Pulaski, Wabash and White counties. Since the northwest swamps were being drained and now settled, the Hammond Deanery embraced Lake and Porter counties. The Fort Wayne and South Bend deaneries took up the rest of the counties of the diocese. The 1903 synod's decrees were published in Latin, German and Polish.

The United States Steel Corporation in 1903 had settled and founded Gary, East Chicago, Indiana Harbor, Hammond, and Whiting, Lake County, and with Inland Steel Corporation contributed to parish buildings. The synod of 1903 was the last Indiana church assembly to enact Cincinnati Provincial and Baltimore Plenary Conciliar

◆ *Father Bernard Kroeger*

decrees. In 1917, St. Pius X promulgated a universal Code of Canon Law for the Church. The United States' bishops had not met since 1884. Thus in 1917, Cardinal James Gibbons, archbishop of Baltimore, used the occasion of World War I to call the bishops together in the National Catholic War Conference. From 1919-1966, the U.S. bishops were organized as the National Catholic Welfare Conference. Bishop Alerding became occupied with the northwestern counties of the diocese around Gary.

DIVERSITY SWELLS THE DIOCESE

U.S. Steel and Inland Steel recruited workers primarily from Eastern Europe and this brought great ethnic diversity to Indiana parishes. On two occasions U.S. Steel gave $50,000 to assist in building parishes. Bishop John Noll's 1941 history records that in one year Bishop Alerding started five parishes in Gary, each of a different nationality.

Pre-World War I circumstances in Europe brought even more immigrants to Indiana. The 1900 U.S. Census shows Indiana had 413,291 German, 128,846 Irish, 58,563 British, 26,266 Canadian, 25,572 French, 14,831 Swiss and Swedish, 10,171 Polish, 10,000 Italian, Russian, Jewish,

◆ *Father John Kubacki, Temperance crusader*

Slovak, Hungarian and Greek ethnic groups among others. Polish people settled in Lake, Porter, LaPorte and St. Joseph counties; some spread to Allen and Madison counties. Italians had settled in Marion County, and while many were occupied in produce distribution, Cass County's stone quarries attracted a contingent at Logansport. At Logansport, they were associated with St. Vincent de Paul Church, especially after the Germans built St. Joseph Church (1869) during the Temperance Crusade years when Father Bernard Kroeger built an English-speaking St. Bridget Church on the town's west side (1875). Though many ethnic groups were associated with and some dominated in parishes now in the Diocese of Lafayette-in-Indiana, St. Boniface, Lafayette (1853), was the only parish officially erected for an ethnic group.

Prior to World War I, the American Protective Association had harassed Catholics. From 1886-1902, its goals were to make English a prerequisite for American citizenship, to remove Catholics from teaching in public schools or holding public office, and to claim that the Knights of Labor were part of a conspiracy against American institutions. The association saw to it that Catholic Indian schools such as the one at Rensselaer went federally unfunded and closed. Though the APA became politically incorrect and faded by World War I, its echoes continued in the second Ku Klux Klan that arose in Georgia in 1915. (The first Ku Klux Klan after the War Between the States was an anti-black reactionary hate group functioning from 1866 to 1871. The second Ku Klux Klan, 1915-1944, was not only anti-black, but also anti-Jewish, anti-Catholic and anti-immigrant.)

At World War I, Indiana Germans spontaneously recognized that they were American. This was symbolized by changing the Indianapolis monument of Germania's name to Columbia. At St. Boniface, Lafayette, in 1918, Father Florian Broede shocked the congregation with the announcement that German would no longer be spoken in church or school!

MISSION STATUS ENDS AND URBANIZATION BEGINS

I RONICALLY in 1908, just when Bishop Alerding was at a loss for priests to serve many ethnic groups, the Roman Congregation for the Propagation of the Faith removed the United States from its status as a mission country. Until this time priests were ordained "to the title of the mission" and could be moved easily. Now they were ordained "to a diocese." United States dioceses were expected to become self-supporting and to take their turn in contributing to the Church's missions in other places.

The Catholic Foreign Mission Society of America was thus founded in 1911 at Maryknoll, New York. The Catholic Church Extension Society at Chicago was founded in 1905 to evangelize the still unchurched areas in the United States. The Bureau of Catholic Indian Missions started in 1874 and had been made a permanent organization at the 1884 Plenary Council of Baltimore, which set up the Commission for Catholic Missions among Colored People and the Indians in 1885.

There was also a social reaction to the urban lifestyle that industrialization had produced. After World War I, several national organizations arose to support the fading rural lifestyle. In the Catholic corner, Monsignor Luigi Ligutti promoted rural life as the solution to urbanization and industrialization from 1920-1950. His early rhetoric repeated motifs from secular organizations, but with a religious theme extolling nature's gifts and God's creation. This sentiment still affects the modern country life mindset that gives expensive subdivisions names such as Smiths Farms, Glowing Glades, and so on.

A priest of the archdiocese of St. Paul-Minneapolis, Father Edwin O'Hara, director of the Rural Life Bureau of the National Catholic Welfare Conference, 1920-1930, founded the National Catholic Rural Life Conference in 1923 to focus on rural parishes and to provide services and advocacy for rural communities that were being transformed into a suburban lifestyle. After Bishop Alerding's death at 79 on December 6, 1924, from injuries sustained when a streetcar rammed his car on Thanksgiving Day, Bishop John Noll introduced an NCRL director to the diocese.

In 1922 with the help of U.S. Steel, the Bishop Alerding-Judge Gary Settlement House was established. Thus, not only Gary, but South Bend, Fort Wayne and northern Indiana reflected the transition to the industrial age. Actually, the entire Great Lakes region developed extensive industrial centers with large ethnic populations that eventually spread satellites into Lafayette, Kokomo, Marion, Muncie, Anderson and Logansport. Even blacks and Mexicans migrated to take unskilled jobs and were used as strike breakers in labor union disputes. Southern women came to work as domestics and seamstresses. People in urban and rural areas lived in ghettos in a very segregated society. After World War I, the U.S. Congress enacted legislation to reduce immigration.

BISHOP NOLL RISES TO THE OCCASION

BECAUSE most immigrants to Indiana were Catholic, the second Ku Klux Klan found fertile ground for its agenda. In 1923, Klan promoter D. C. Stephenson, who had senatorial and presidential aspirations, held his inauguration as grand dragon at Kokomo's Malfalfa Park. A Klan internal conflict led Stephenson to continue as grand dragon of his own Independent Klan of America, which elected Indiana's governor, the Indianapolis mayor, and other officials. While Indiana's legislature was deadlocked, and numerous Catholic businessmen suffered political recriminations, things began to fall apart in 1925 when Stephenson was arrested and charged with the murder of Madge Oberholtzer, then convicted and sentenced to life imprisonment. Since no political pardons came his way, Stephenson exposed the Klan's activities. The Indianapolis mayor and a Muncie judge fell out of office as the organization deteriorated.

These movements galvanized Father John Noll. While at Immaculate Conception Church, Kendallville, 1900-1902, taking care of its missions at Ligonier, Millersburg, Albion and Rome City, he became interested in dialogue with non-Catholics. During his assignment to St. Louis Church, Besancon, he received permission to spend a year conducting lecture courses to non-Catholics throughout northern

◆ *Bishop Noll*

Indiana. In 1903, "Kind Words from Your Pastor" opened a literary career that became a magazine when Father Noll was at St. John the Evangelist Church, Hartford City, in 1908. When he went to Huntington in 1912, a national Catholic weekly publication, Our Sunday Visitor, was born. Father Noll also founded The Acolyte, a continuing education periodical for the clergy. Among his many publications, "Father Smith Instructs Jackson" became very popular.

Monsignor Noll was chosen as the fifth Bishop of Fort Wayne and installed in the Cathedral of the Immaculate Conception on June 30, 1925. With Our Sunday Visitor income, he built a Training School and Novitiate for Missionary Catechists on a knoll outside Huntington. In 1928, this religious congregation, founded by Father J. J. Sigstein of Chicago, became recognized as the Missionary Catechists of Our Lady of Victory Noll. Their main apostolate was to Mexicans settled in the United States southwest. But they also came as catechists to many parishes in northern Indiana, particularly in northern Jasper, Newton and Cass counties.

Bishop Noll also used his enterprise's proceeds for home and foreign missions. His disbursements went to seminary education funds at Maryknoll, the Venard Institute, the Catholic Church Extension Society, as well as to Victory Noll. Small wonder he became executive secretary of the American Board of Catholic Missions.

EFFECTIVE PARISH INNOVATIONS

P RIOR to Father Noll, church announcements were made aloud before the final blessing at Mass. He instituted printing a Sunday bulletin, which was revolutionary. Letters came to the bishop from parishioners protesting that their Mass intentions were not announced, but posted on a church door bulletin board. But with so many now attending parochial school, even Catholic high school, the bishop was confident that parishioners could read. This was, in fact, the very reason Father Noll's literary apostolate became so important. When he became fifth Bishop of Fort Wayne in 1925, he founded the diocesan newspaper, The Harmonizer, which included Our Sunday Visitor as a supplement. This began a trend in which many dioceses had Huntington publish their diocesan newspaper or an edition that inserted Our Sunday Visitor.

Introducing the collection envelope was another innovation Father Noll made through his apostolate. Indeed, the traditional practice of supporting the Church, the priests, and the works of charity with the "first fruits" of the harvest had long included gifts other than money. People bartered among themselves prior to paper money becoming standardized as worth its tender at the turn of the century. Thus, charging "pew rent" or meeting workers outside a factory before they spent any of their wages, or holding bazaars and raffles as if they were the Church's main mission could be replaced by this orderly way of Church support. And so, Our Sunday Visitor began taking orders to print envelopes for other parishes and dioceses for contribution envelopes. This became a common practice in the United States.

When Bishop Noll held a 1926 synod, it decreed Church support was to come from Sunday Mass collections (No. 142). Interestingly, two subsequent decrees are the only ones that retain reference to the Third Plenary Council of Baltimore forbidding picnics, excursions, lawn festivals, and the like without the bishop's permission (No. 143). Fairs, banquets, and socials in the church basement while Mass was in progress upstairs were not allowed, and card playing and dancing absolutely forbidden (No. 144).

SUBURBAN LIFESTYLE GROWS

D URING this time, roads began to be built. Ever since Elwood Haynes, one of Indiana's car inventors, had taken his seven-mile drive down Pumpkin Pike at Kokomo in 1894, county commissioners were purchasing and paving roads. The state took to paving state roads, and federal transportation departments began laying out Interstate highways. With cars and trucks, people could go where trains could not, including to church.

Already in 1900, Bishop Alerding had consolidated the Boxley and Arcadia missions into Sacred Heart of Jesus Church, Cicero. People from Noblesville's closed St. Vincent de Paul Church in 1906 could take the Interurban there. Bishop Alerding sent Father Charles McCabe to Otterbein in 1902 to build St. Charles Borromeo Church that made the Barrydale countryside church its mission in 1931 till its 1991 closing. This same Father McCabe was sent to Gas City's St. Genevieve Church of the Gas Boom era (1893) to replace it with Holy Family Church (1910). Bishop Alerding also dedicated SS. Peter and Paul Church (1913) at Goodland, which had brought St. Anthony parishioners from the countryside into town. He dedicated a south Kokomo mission of St. Joan of Arc (1922) and St. Joseph Hospital there.

MINISTRIES OF CHARITY

M INISTRY to the sick was a work of charity. At Anderson's St. John Hickey Memorial Hospital (1894), the Sisters of the Holy Cross ran St. John School of Nursing from 1910-1972. At Elwood, the Sisters of St. Joseph of Tipton opened Mercy Hospital in 1926. At Kokomo, they instituted St. Joseph Hospital in 1935. There they also conducted a School of Nursing from 1952-1969. This was in conjunction with the former Good Samaritan Hospital, which was run as a nursing home from 1921-1970.

At Logansport, the Sisters of St. Francis Seraph of Perpetual Adoration operated St. Joseph Hospital, 1893-1974. They also ran St. Anthony Home for the Aged, Lafayette, 1897-1960, in addition to St. Elizabeth Hospital functioning since their arrival in 1876. St. Elizabeth Hospital also began a School of Nursing in conjunction with St. Francis College. From 1906-1924, St. Ann Hospital, Peru, was conducted by the Sisters of St. Francis of Maryville under the auspices of the Wabash Railroad Company primarily for its workers.

Bishop Noll's Dedications and Missions

Bishop Noll's administration opened at the height of post-World War I prosperity. People owned cars and enjoyed freedom to travel. Higher wages, lower prices, installment buying, and technical innovations promoted suburban lifestyles. Whereas in 1900 only 800 cars had been produced, in 1929 almost 27 million cars rode the highways. Factory jobs produced and maintained them. Radio and silent film entertainment captivated popular interest. Rural electrification transformed the countryside by 1930 when almost half the United States population now lived in cities. The resultant mobility and social communication bred an awareness of pluralism heightened by the 1929 Great Depression when people were forced to seek aid outside ethnic or fraternal associations that had collapsed.

Reflecting that Eli Lilly Company, Indianapolis, and Ball Corporation, Muncie, were the only two employers in Indiana that could pay wages during the Great Depression's start, Bishop Noll founded St. Mary Church, Muncie, in 1930. He also dedicated St. Peter Church, Winamac, that year. In 1931, he dedicated St. Charles Borromeo School, Peru. Having dedicated Mercy Hospital, Elwood, in 1926, at Kokomo he also dedicated St. Joseph Hospital's new building in 1936. In 1939, he dedicated a new building at Saint Joseph's College, Rensselaer, and in 1940 he dedicated

St. Augustine Church, Rensselaer, and another new college building. That year he rededicated a renovated Sacred Heart of Jesus Church, Fowler. At Montpelier he dedicated St. Margaret Church on June 10, 1941.

When St. Joseph Orphan Asylum and Manual Labor School, Lafayette, closed in 1937, Bishop Noll transferred its child placement and family relief services to diocesan Catholic Charities. Catholic Charities centers were located at Fort Wayne, South Bend and Hammond.

Of the religious communities, Bishop Noll welcomed the Redemptorist Fathers to St. Joseph, Lebanon, Boone County, and the Cicero mission, Hamilton County. In 1943, the Missionaries of the Company of Mary of St. Louis de Montfort opened Marybrook Novitiate, Hartford City, Blackford County. These Missionaries were assigned the Noblesville mission.

Bishop Noll promoted the Council of Catholic Women, which was to coordinate all parish women's groups, and the Catholic Youth Organization. His literary apostolate spearheaded a national campaign against indecent literature in 1938. The NCWC selected him with three other bishops to launch the Legion of Decency aimed at motion pictures that by now had become talking movies. He was on the board of governors of the Catholic Church Extension Society for 25 years. From 1925 until near his death, he was treasurer of the American Board of Catholic Missions. From 1934-1937,

◆ *Saint Joseph's College, Rensselaer*

A History of the Diocese of Lafayette-in-Indiana

◈ *Saint Joseph's College Chapel*

◈ *St. Joseph's Orphanage, Lafayette*

he was chairman of the NCWC Lay Organizations Department for the Councils of Catholic Women and Catholic Men. Through Our Sunday Visitor, he raised funds to erect a statue of Christ the Light of the World outside the NCWC building in Washington, D.C., and collected funds for the National Shrine of the Immaculate Conception at the Catholic University of America campus. Pope Pius XII gave him the personal title of archbishop in 1953.

OPTIMISM AFTER WORLD WAR II

THOUGH the Depression years had been trying, great optimism after World War II transformed the Midwest industrial centers. Its factories and farms were major contributors to the war's success and thrived on the subsequent Cold War. Women and mixed ethnic groups in the work force developed social pluralism. The Detroit automobile industry located many satellite plants in northern Indiana cities such as Lafayette, Kokomo, Marion, Muncie, Anderson and in many smaller towns. After World War II, National Homes headquartered at Lafayette produced housing for returning veterans settling into new suburbs that began dotting cities and towns. The war had heightened Church participation, which was reflected by increased Catholic school attendance and religious vocations.

Pope Pius XII created new dioceses in all the Midwest's Church provinces: Chicago, Milwaukee, Cincinnati and Detroit. In the Cincinnati Province, which had included Indiana since 1850, Archbishop Timothy McNicholas was in his latter days. In a 1980 history of Our Lady of Mt. Carmel Parish, Father Michael Kettron reports that Archbishop McNicholas was the national moderator of the National Catholic Rural Life Conference at this time. Older people had given him the thought that it would be beneficial to have a basically rural diocese as he perceived Indiana in comparison with Cincinnati.

Whatever perceptions Archbishop McNicholas may have had, Bishop Noll was aware of Lafayette's status, as recorded in his own 1941 history, The Diocese of Fort Wayne, Fragments of History. He accepted Archbishop McNicholas' decision to constitute Fort Wayne's southern three deaneries of Lafayette, Logansport and Muncie into the Diocese of Lafayette-in-Indiana. In fact, in an April 19, 1930, letter, Bishop Noll wrote to his nephew Father John Dillon at Lafayette, "Six years ago, splitting the diocese was anticipated." That is, at the time of Bishop Alerding's death, Lafayette was destined for a bishopric. Thus, in 1944 the Diocese of Indianapolis was made a metropolitan see with Fort Wayne, Evansville and Lafayette-in-Indiana as its suffragan dioceses.

The Diocese of Lafayette-in-Indiana was officially established on Oct. 21, 1944.

Holy Trinity Church, Bryant

Chapter 4

LAFAYETTE-IN-INDIANA: A NEW DIOCESE

ARCHBISHOP Joseph Ritter of Indianapolis installed Bishop John George Bennett as first Bishop of Lafayette-in-Indiana on January 18, 1945, in Lafayette's Cathedral of St. Mary of the Immaculate Conception. It was an optimistic era. From 1945-1970, Indiana experienced recovery from the Great Depression and a post-World War II prosperity from the automobile industry such as it had not seen since its late 19th century northern colonization. By mid-20th century, farms were mechanized. With urban and suburban migrations, agribusiness began replacing family farms.

Although people continued to live in the countryside, they commuted to work in nearby town factories. The Pennsylvania Turnpike had been built in 1940 to ease rural traffic; but by President Dwight Eisenhower's administration (1953-1961), Congress had enacted support of a national interstate system that heralded the railroads' demise. In addition, aviation introduced fast public and private travel.

The post-World War II optimism saw the United Nations organize international relations into today's awareness of the global village. The National Catholic Welfare Conference (NCWC) developed Catholic Charities to professionalize the Church's service to the poor and founded the St. Vincent de Paul Society in the United States. The NCWC also pioneered the National Conference of Catholic Women to unify women's former sodalities, circles, and societies. The National Council of Catholic Men was launched with a similar purpose. As public schools began losing their Protestant character, the Confraternity of Christian Doctrine, established in the 1920s, was given impetus as an outreach to children not attending parochial schools. In fact, so many returning veterans were attending secular institutions under the G.I. Bill that the Church lifted the ban on Catholics attending them and promoted Catholic student chapels.

BISHOP BENNETT BEGINS

FATHER John Bennett was a product of his times. He had been born at Dunnington, Benton County, January 20, 1891. He grew up in Holy Trinity Parish (renamed Nativity of the Blessed Virgin Mary in 1893) where Father Francis Lambert served from 1888-1918.

◆ Bishop Bennett Consecration

◆ 1950 Diocesan council of Catholic nurses

◆ 1951 Diocesan Retreat

◆ Bishop Bennett

At the parochial school, he was taught by the Sisters of St. Francis Seraph of Perpetual Adoration from Lafayette. After attending Saint Joseph's College, Rensselaer, he entered St. Meinrad Seminary, and was ordained a priest on June 27, 1914, by Bishop Herman Alerding at Fort Wayne's Cathedral of the Immaculate Conception.

His first assignment was to one of Fort Wayne's prosperous parishes at that time, St. Patrick. He was with the distinguished Father John Delaney whose achievements brought him the title of a monsignor in 1928, the year Father Bennett was transferred to be pastor of SS. Peter and Paul Church, Garrett. At the virtual suburb of Fort Wayne, Father Bennett activated a building fund his predecessor had started that resulted in the Romanesque-style brick St. Joseph Church and rectory. The Sisters of the Sacred Heart of St. Francis taught in St. Joseph's parochial school and administered a hospital there.

At St. Joseph, Father Bennett donated a mural of St. Anne teaching the Virgin Mary and a window depicting the Good Shepherd. The parish children donated a sacristy window depicting St. Aloysius in honor of Father Bennett. At the same time, he commuted to Fort Wayne as a Defender of the Bond in the diocesan matrimonial tribunal. In 1941,

Bishop Noll named him Dean of the Fort Wayne Deanery and gave him the title of monsignor. When the creation of the Diocese of Lafayette-in-Indiana was announced in October 1944, less than a month later Msgr. Bennett was appointed its bishop.

Bishop Noll ordained Msgr. Bennett a bishop January 10, 1945, at Fort Wayne. In his August 22, 1956, welcome to his Coadjutor Bishop John Carberry and near the end of his time, Bishop Bennett remarked, "If there should be among you a young man who has aspirations to be the first bishop of a diocese, let him think carefully over this matter and prayerfully hope that it never happens to him."

INTO THE LORD'S VINEYARD

BISHOP Bennett went into the 9,832 square miles of his new diocese encouraged by the Catholic Rural Life Conference to strengthen rural life at the very time the new diocese was becoming suburbanized. With acumen reflecting his background, he appointed directors of many diocesan offices, but none to a rural life office. It was not until 1958 that his successor Bishop Carberry appointed Father Francis Scheck the diocese's first director of the Rural Life program.

Previous chapters have listed how countryside churches closed or were consolidated starting in 1900. Some moved into towns. Second churches were established in larger cities such as Kokomo (1922), Muncie (1930) and Anderson (1947). Bishop Bennett himself began parishes in Noblesville (1945), Monticello (1952), Carmel (1955), West Lafayette St. Thomas (1951) and Blessed Sacrament (1957). He closed the mission churches at Veedersburg (1946), Redkey (1949), and Fairmount (1950), and made parishes of missions at Wheatfield (1945), Francesville (1946), Medaryville (1949), and Lucerne (1953).

The suburbanization of the diocese continued in force in the 1960s as people migrated from Chicago and Lake County to the diocese's northern counties: Newton, Jasper, Pulaski, White and Fulton, and as people moved north from Marion County to Montgomery, Boone, Hamilton and Madison counties. People from rural areas came either to work or to live in neighboring cities. For example, residents of Benton, Carroll, Warren, Montgomery and Fountain counties came to Lafayette. Even those actually doing agribusiness began functioning through major business suppliers and modern technology.

Yet the diocese's Rural Life program persisted into the 1980s until the present reality was recognized. Father Frederick Gschwind was the diocese's second and last appointed Rural Life director, although he had not been active in that role for many years. In his column dated June 20, 2005, on the diocese's 60th anniversary, Bishop William Higi observed the irony of Bishop Bennett dedicating a large, new church at rural Dunnington in 1952 that today serves 80 households, while in 1955 he had the foresight, despite opposition from some clergy, to establish Our Lady of Mt. Carmel, a suburban parish that today serves more than 2,800 households.

EARLY DIOCESAN ORGANIZATION

THE Franciscan Sisters provided Bishop Bennett a temporary apartment at St. Elizabeth Hospital until he could purchase and move into the 610 Lingle Avenue residence on March 1, 1945. In a little office space at the hospital, then at the bishop's residence, his chancery began with Betty Carroll at the typewriter and Father Emil Schweier as chancellor and tribunal notary. Father John Dillon of St. Ann Church, Lafayette, was the tribunal judge. Bishop Bennett appointed Msgr. Thomas Travers, Anderson, his vicar general, 1945-1955, when he retired to San Diego, California; and Msgr. Felix Seroczynski, Muncie, 1955-1956.

◈ *Bishop Bennett with Father Niesen, 1949, at Kokomo*

On Jan. 21, 1945, Our Sunday Visitor, Huntington, provided a Lafayette Edition. Since all priests serving in a diocesan office worked from their own residences, the Lafayette Edition's editor Father James Quinn, chaplain at St. Joseph Hospital, Kokomo, with residence at St. Joan of Arc rectory, typed his copy and mailed it to Huntington from there. Father Henry Ward, Crawfordsville, served as the paper's business manager until 1957.

On Dec. 1, 1947, Bishop Bennett announced a Diocesan Building Fund for a Chancery building. His letter mentions it would alleviate working in the dining room, hall, or living room of the bishop's residence. It took until 1955 to complete the Chancery building for use as diocesan offices.

MINISTRIES UNFOLD

BISHOP Bennett's first confirmations were for U.S. Navy personnel at Purdue University on February 18, 1945, and at Bunker Hill Naval Air Station in Miami County on March 2, 1945. On February 2, 1945, he ordained Fathers Donald Hardebeck, George Lanning, Charles Muller and Richard Puetz, and on August 16, Father Harold Weller to the priesthood at the Cathedral of St. Mary of the Immaculate Conception. His first parish confirmations were at St. Mary, Dunnington, on April 10, 1945. He returned to St. Joseph, Garrett, on Nov. 21 that year to confirm 51 children and 13 adults.

When the Missionaries of the Company of Mary of St. Louis de Montfort organized a mission chapel at Noblesville, Bishop Bennett offered the first Mass in Our Lady of Grace Chapel there on December 6, 1945. The following May 19 he dedicated Noblesville's first Our Lady of Grace Church. On property the Pursley family had donated to the diocese at Hartford City, these missionaries opened a novitiate in 1949.

People had been left with only the 1884 Baltimore Catechism that catechized them for first Communion and confirmation, and there developed need for more adult formation. Bishop Bennett organized the Te Deum International adult formation program at Lafayette, March 3, 1946, and instituted it at Logansport, April 27, 1946. Also in 1946, he consecrated the diocese to Jesus through the Immaculate Heart of Mary.

It was a historic occasion on August 23-25, 1949, when Bishop Bennett hosted the first national convention of the National Clergy Conference on Alcoholism at Rensselaer. Among four priests responsible for organizing this conference, in service today as the National Catholic Council on Alcoholism and Related Drug Problems, was Father John Dillon, Lafayette.

ILLNESS BRINGS ASSISTANCE

ALREADY on Oct. 30, 1949, prayers were requested for Bishop Bennett's health. The public announcement was made that he was advised to ease his schedule. Despite his illness, which proved to be years in duration, the first bishop continued to build up the diocese with lasting effect with other bishops' assistance.

In April 2, 1950, Bishop Charles Helmsing of Kansas City came to Lafayette to consecrate the holy oils at the Chrism Mass. On May 7, Archbishop Paul Schulte of Indianapolis dedicated the new St. Joan of Arc Church,

◆ Bishop Bennett funeral

Kokomo. On May 25, Bishop Charles LeBlond of St. Joseph, Missouri, ordained Father Michael Reineck. On November 19, Bishop Bennett was able to bless the new St. John the Baptist School, Tipton. In 1951, Bishop Bennett was able to administer confirmation only in January and May at St. Elizabeth Hospital Chapel, Lafayette, and at St. Thomas Aquinas Chapel, West Lafayette, respectively. Archbishop Schulte substituted for confirmations at nine parishes during October, and Fort Wayne Auxiliary Bishop Leo Pursley administered confirmation at Hartford City in December.

Bishop Bennett rallied and was able to continue a full confirmation schedule until 1956. He announced a missionary plan for the diocese on March 11, 1951. A map published on September 30 showed the diocese was only 6 percent Catholic. In addition to the Montfort Missionaries at Noblesville, the Congregation of the Most Holy Redeemer (Redemptorists) from Lebanon had been visiting Zionsville since 1945. There, property was purchased in 1948 for the start of St. Alphonsus Liguori Church.

In 1955, January 8 saw the announcement of Bishop Bennett's sudden illness of a heart condition. On May 3, Cincinnati Auxiliary Bishop Clarence Issenmann ordained Fathers William Grady, James Keane, Edward Matuszak, James O'Neill, Joseph Ruffing, and Donald Vernon at the Lafayette Cathedral. This was the same year Bishop Bennett arranged for the Sisters Adorers of the Precious Blood to found their monastery at Lafayette on March 21. On September 5, he blessed the new Marion Bennett High School at St. Paul Parish. St. Francis High School for Girls closed on June 1 making it possible for the girls to continue at the new co-educational Lafayette Central Catholic High School for which Bishop Bennett broke ground on July 22, 1956.

TRANSITION TO A SECOND BISHOP

BISHOP Bennett entered St. Elizabeth Hospital, Lafayette, January 15, 1956. During this year groundbreaking for a new St. Joseph Convent Motherhouse was held at Tipton. Our Lady of Mt. Carmel Church was built. On March 4, a statewide diocesan census was announced; on April 2, the first biannual Catholic Youth Organization convention was held. On May 9, it was announced that Msgr. John Carberry of the Diocese of Brooklyn was appointed coadjutor bishop with right of succession to Bishop Bennett. Bishop Pursley presided at the 1956 ordinations to the priesthood. Coadjutor Bishop

◈ *Cardinal Carberry*

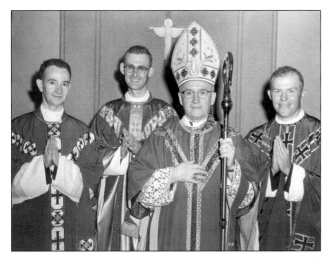

◈ *Fathers Smith, Higi and Gross ordained by Bishop Carberry, 1959*

◈ *Community of the Monastery of the Precious Blood*

◈ *Indiana Bishops Grimmelsman, Bennett, Schulte and Pursley welcome Bishop Carberry*

◈ *Central Catholic High School, Lafayette*

◈ *Monastery of the Precious Blood, Lafayette*

Bishop Bennett greets Bishop Carberry at the Lafayette train station, August 1956

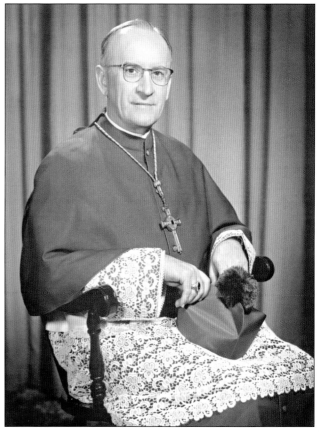

Bishop Carberry

Carberry was received at Lafayette on Aug. 22, 1956, and appointed pastor of the Cathedral of St. Mary of the Immaculate Conception and Bishop Bennett's vicar general. While at the Cathedral, Bishop Carberry introduced the perpetual novena to Our Lady of the Miraculous Medal. His devotion to the Blessed Virgin Mary permeated his ministry in the diocese and other dioceses, which he served until his death on June 17, 1998.

While Bishop Carberry conducted the dedications of Our Lady of Mt. Carmel Church, Carmel, September 16, 1956, and the Broderick Memorial Building at St. Mary School, Muncie, September 23, Bishop Bennett presided at the Lafayette Central Catholic High School cornerstone laying on October 21. But by March 10, 1957, Bishop Bennett was back in St. Elizabeth Hospital. Coadjutor Bishop Carberry held the 1957 ordinations to the priesthood at the Cathedral. Bishop Bennett's Oct. 20, 1957, return to Lafayette Central Catholic High School was his final dedication. On November 20, at age 66, he died at St. Elizabeth Hospital. Following the funeral in the Cathedral, his body was buried in St. Mary Cemetery.

In bidding Coadjutor Bishop Carberry a warm welcome on August 22, 1956, Bishop Bennett summarized the

diocese at that point in history when he said, "We cannot offer him the vast number of spiritual children that his former diocese contains, but we can and do offer him a devoted clergy, a self-sacrificing religious family, and a laity that is, to my mind, the salt of the earth. In good time he will learn to know all of the elements of the diocese as well as I know them, and I am convinced he will appreciate their loyalty as I do."

BISHOP CARBERRY CARRIES ON

ON June 29, 1958, Bishop Carberry dedicated a third St. Bernard Church, Crawfordsville, when the parish relocated from Pike and Washington streets to a suburban section of town in the 1300 block of East Main Street. On October 29, Bishop Carberry held the first synod of the diocese to implement the 1917 Code of Canon Law and published its decrees on May 10, 1959. Bishop Carberry had doctorates in philosophy and theology from Roman universities, where he prepared for his ordination to the priesthood on July 28, 1929. His 1934 doctorate in canon law from The Catholic University of America, Washington, D.C., enabled him to facilitate the synod expeditiously. Besides, he had just finished a 1955-

Bishop Carberry Installation, Columbus

Bishop Carberry at the Diocesan Synod

Bishop Carberry leaves Lafayette

1956 term as president of the Canon Law Society of America while serving as judge on the Brooklyn diocesan tribunal, teaching part-time at the diocesan seminary, and doing health care chaplaincy when he was made coadjutor bishop to Bishop Bennett. The synod's decrees were received with demur in light of the January 25, 1959, announcement by Blessed John XXIII that there was to be an ecumenical council at the Vatican. There was expectation that changes would be coming.

The Chancery building was completed. Bishop Carberry transferred several offices into its facilities and initiated a more systematic central diocesan administration. On March 21, 1958, he incorporated the diocese under state non-profit organization laws.

Bishop Carberry invited the Poor Clare nuns to the diocese and on March 19, 1959, he had his vicar general Msgr. John Schall dedicate their monastery at Kokomo. In 1960, the St. Vincent de Paul Society was organized in the diocese. In 1961, he blessed cornerstones at new churches at Monticello, July 9, and West Lafayette, July 23. He dedicated the Church of the Blessed Sacrament, West Lafayette, April 1, 1962; Our Lady of the Lakes, Monticello, May 27; and St. Ambrose, Anderson, December 16. The Council of Catholic Men was established in 1962. On

Bishop Carberry with Pope John XXIII

September 19, that year, he welcomed the Victory Noll Catechist Sisters to the diocese for religious education in Newton, Jasper, Pulaski, Fulton and Cass counties. Msgr. Schall administered the diocese while the bishop attended the Second Vatican Council Oct. 11-December 8, 1962; September 29-December 4, 1963; and September 14-November 21, 1964.

GROWTH AND CHANGE

O N March 15, 1964, Bishop Carberry announced that a census would be conducted on November 15. Although most of this census material has been destroyed, some mimeographed circulars retained from the Notre Dame Sociology Department that administered it describe the diocese as 60 percent urban or suburban, 15 percent in towns, and just 25 percent rural of a total Catholic population of 73,822. When Bishop Carberry became second Bishop of Lafayette-in-Indiana, a December 1957 Indianapolis News article headlined:

◆ Postulants received into Sisters of St. Joseph of Tipton, 1959

"Rural Diocese is Revelation to New Bishop." The census revealed that at last the diocese had in fact developed a suburban pattern.

Also, the diocese increased from 45 parishes with a resident pastor to 56. Of the 38,991 people aged 18 and older who had completed any schooling in 1964, Bishop

◆ Saint Joseph's College Chapel, 1951

Carberry's census found 35,155 had attended Catholic schools. Of 23,752 children actually in public or parochial grades 1-12 in 1964, it found 9,456 attending Catholic schools in September 1965. From its 31,700 population reported in the 1945 Catholic Directory, the diocese in 1965 had grown to 73,521 Catholics.

On January 20, 1965, the announcement was made that Bishop Carberry had been transferred to the Diocese of Columbus. He dedicated a new Immaculate Conception Church, Portland, Feb. 7, before his departure from Lafayette on March 19. Msgr. Schall was elected diocesan administrator.

◈ *St. Joseph Academy Graduation, 1952*

◈ *Sisters of St. Joseph trip to Ireland, 1948*

◆ *Second Vatican Council.*
Photo courtesy CNS

Chapter 5

DEVELOPMENTS AND CHANGES

◆ *Bishop Carberry at Vatican II*

◆ *Bishop Carberry with Msgr. Schall*

BY mid-20th century the Church had developed to a place of hoping to influence American society for the better. Traditional Catholic ethnic groups – Irish, German, Italian, and Slavic – had entered the cultural mainstream symbolized by President John Kennedy's 1960 election.

At the same time, the Church in the United States experienced both social and ecclesial changes. Parishes had more educated and financially successful people. The so-called baby-boomers matured in a culture characterized by quests for racial equality, women's advancement and a technological revolution in media and communication. A massive nonviolent march on Washington, D.C., against poverty and racism in March 1963 was followed by Congress' enactment of the 1964 Civil Rights Act. On November 22, 1963, President Kennedy was assassinated. Extensive racial riots erupted in 1965, especially at Watts, California, and in 1967 at Detroit. Even more riots dotted the country at Dr. Martin Luther King Jr.'s assassination on April 4, 1968. Meanwhile peace movements, especially among university students, protested the Vietnam conflict. The Weatherman riots in Chicago in October 1969 were the most violent.

Many Catholic religious and some diocesan clergy, even laity, became openly involved in the demonstrations for racial equality and peace. In 1972-1977, Indiana repealed the death penalty as a form of capital punishment.

By 1965, the Midwest, including Indiana, had been enjoying the height of industrial prosperity as well as suffering travails of social change. Abortion was illegal, people rallied for world peace and mass movements protested racial inequality and poverty in America. In Indiana, ethnic groups with jobs and new prosperity were able to relocate readily. "White flight" became a recognizable phenomenon.

THE DIOCESE'S THIRD BISHOP ARRIVES

AS the Second Vatican Council was completed in 1962-1965, the National Catholic Welfare Conference reorganized into the National Conference of Catholic Bishops (for Church matters) and

Bishop Gallagher

Bishop Gallagher in Rome for Vatican II

Blessed John XXIII Center, 1991

the United States Catholic Conference (for public affairs) in 1966. In 1997, these would be combined into the United States Conference of Catholic Bishops. The National Conference of Catholic Charities was also being revised.

Amid these events, Pope Paul VI appointed Msgr. Raymond Gallagher third Bishop of Lafayette-in-Indiana. He had been executive secretary of the National Conference of Catholic Charities, Washington, D.C., since 1961. A priest of the Diocese of Cleveland, the 52-year-old Msgr. Gallagher was ordained a bishop by the apostolic delegate Archbishop Amleto Ciccognani at Cleveland Cathedral of St. John the Evangelist on August 11, 1965. After Archbishop Paul Schulte of Indianapolis installed Bishop Gallagher in Lafayette's Cathedral of St. Mary of

the Immaculate Conception on August 23, Bishop Gallagher left on September 2 to attend the fourth and final session of the Second Vatican Council from September 14 to December 8, 1965. He appointed his vicar general, Msgr. John Schall, in charge of the diocese in his absence. Intense media interest in this Council was reflected in a grand welcome back from Rome for Bishop Gallagher at the Lafayette Cathedral on December 10.

VATICAN COUNCIL IMPLEMENTATION BEGINS

AFTER dedicating the new St. Joseph Hall, Winchester, on June 12, 1966, Bishop Gallagher made known his July 11 purchase of Lake Freeman property at Monticello, White County, to be used as Paul VI Retreat Center. After his August 14 announcement of plans to implement the Council, Bishop Gallagher dedicated a donated house in Hartford City, Blackford County, as John XXIII Retreat Center. Father Patrick Keith Hosey was named its director. Initially it provided retreat programs to present Bishop Gallagher's stated purpose to provide ongoing adult formation in Conciliar implementation. This center continues after Father Hosey's 2006 retirement to be a place where people of all faiths are welcome to programs in the spirit of Vatican II. It is directed by Poor Handmaid of Jesus Christ Sister Joetta Huelsmann.

Recognizing the population migrations that had occurred in northern Newton, Jasper, Pulaski and White counties as well as in the diocese's southern Boone, Hamilton and Madison counties, on December 22, 1968, Bishop Gallagher created three new deaneries: Anderson (Madison, Grant, Hamilton and Tipton counties) from the Muncie Deanery; Fowler (Benton, Jasper and Newton counties) from the Lafayette Deanery; and Monticello (Carroll, Pulaski and White counties) from the Logansport Deanery.

On November 17, after he dedicated the new Bennett Hall at the Church of the Blessed Sacrament, West Lafayette, he traveled to Kokomo to address a diocesan Catholic Youth Organization convention. At this time priests were deanery moderators coordinating parish youth organizations. While in other assignments Fathers Charles Muller, 1952-1964; Thomas Fox, 1964-1970; and Thomas Timmerman, 1970-1975, had directed CYO's many activities. In 1976, Bishop Gallagher made Father Douglas McCormack full-time director of youth ministry. Also, on August 25, 1968, Bishop Gallagher instituted a Christian formation program for adult education.

◆ *25th Anniversary of the Diocese of Lafayette-in-Indiana, 1969*

HUMANAE VITAE

ON July 29, 1968, Pope Paul VI issued an encyclical letter forbidding artificial birth control, Humanae Vitae (On Human Life). While most encyclicals pass quietly into history, this encyclical letter received a controversial media reception and in Catholic circles, including the diocese, its shock waves vibrated. Whereas previous moral teaching had questioned whether a Catholic pharmacist allowing condoms for sale could approach Communion, now the invention of a birth control pill and use of other artificial means came into vogue even among Catholics. Considered in retrospect to be a prophetic encyclical letter, its issues continue to be part of Church moral teaching.

PASTORAL COUNCILS

To apply Vatican II documents to the diocese, Bishop Gallagher convoked a Diocesan Assembly. The results of the Assembly were published January 9, 1969, in a booklet titled "Vatican II and Diocesan Renewal: Assembly Documents, Diocese of Lafayette-in-Indiana, Blueprint for Renewal: Structure of the Parish Council." The Assembly's goal was formation of parish pastoral councils in every parish.

In the Assembly documents preface, Bishop Gallagher wrote, "The priests, religious, and laity of the diocese have addressed themselves to the challenge of making the traditional teachings of the Church fully related to the times in which we are living." If it appears that Church history was heavily clergy- and religious-oriented to this time, it was. Encouragement of the apostolate of the laity is a recent development. The Assembly process had each parish discussing drafts of the 16 documents of Vatican Council II grouped into 12 for study and implementation. Recommended changes were sent to a Preparatory Commission to make a revised draft. Meeting at Lafayette Central Catholic High School, parish representatives worked out the revised drafts returned from a second parish study. Finally, on October 29, 1967, at St. Patrick Church, Kokomo, about 1,000 people gathered to vote on the third and final form of the drafts. Bishop Gallagher accepted these finalized drafts as the people's voice regarding the diocese's application of Vatican II.

To support revised administrative efforts, on January 25, 1969, Bishop Gallagher instituted the Growth Campaign. Through this annual appeal, a former Kokomo estate was purchased in 1970 and diocesan Catholic Charities, religious education, and pastoral council offices were located there. Bishop Gallagher asked Father Louis Heitz, a 1967 graduate of The Catholic University of America's School of Social Services, to reorganize Catholic Charities. Father Heitz maintained his office at the Kokomo site while coordinating Catholic Charities satellite offices at Lafayette and Muncie. Father Charles Kline was appointed religious education director to develop Confraternity of Christian Doctrine programs and resources into education for adults as well as youth. This promoted parishes having religious education directors.

On April 3, 1970, Bishop Gallagher appointed Father Paul Dehner as executive director of the Diocesan Pastoral Council at the Kokomo site. By December 15, 1972, the DPC issued a Parish Pastoral Council Handbook that included detailed parish council procedures, apostolate structures and expectations, as well as DPC and Indiana Catholic Conference information. From 1972, Father Dehner also directed an Office of Information, and from 1975-1978, an Office of Communication. On February 17, 1974, the DPC produced its own Constitution and bylaws. Its chairs were Thomas Medland, 1970-1971; Charles Malady, 1972-1973; Richard Worden, 1974; Patrick Roberts, 1975; Donald Reed, 1976; Anthony Petrucce, 1977; Ronald Anjard, 1978; Genevieve Lasher, 1979; Albert Diener, 1980; and Leo Schifferli, 1981-1982. By numerous maps and materials, the DPC formed its own districts and began referring to an eastern and western diocesan area. It gave Catholics in mission areas a stronger tie with the diocese's vision.

When Father Dehner was appointed pastor of St. Charles Borromeo Church, Peru, in 1978-1981, parish pastoral councils had become a reality. By the time of Bishop Gallagher's 1982 retirement, the DPC demonstrated that it had achieved its goal. Thus when Bishop George Fulcher became the fourth Bishop of Lafayette-in-Indiana in 1983, he did not reconvene it.

DEDICATIONS AND LEADERSHIP

MEANWHILE, on November 27, 1967, St. Mary Church, Frankfort, moved from its Walnut Street site and relocated to the developing east side of town. On August 15, 1968, after Bishop Gallagher consecrated St. Mary Church, Muncie, he dedicated Frankfort's new St. Mary Church on September 8. On September 6, 1969, he dedicated a new Maria Regina Mater Monastery for the Poor Clares at Kokomo. From 1968-1971, an attempt was made to have Monks of the Holy Savior open Holy Trinity Monastery, Hartford City, in the former Marybrook Novitiate of the Company of Mary of St. Louis de Montfort, 1943-1968.

In 1969, Bishop Gallagher was an organizer and co-founder of the Indiana Catholic Conference. At the request of Indianapolis' Archbishops Paul Schulte and George Biskup, he functioned as its executive chair until 1980. On October 14, 1973, he initiated the ICC's Project Priesthood, which was a program familiarizing priests with the ICC's agenda. He also was chair of the Indiana Interreligious Commission on Human Equality, 1967-

◈ *Groundbreaking for a new monastery of the Poor Clares in Kokomo, 1968*

1971. Having served as spiritual director and later episcopal moderator of the Ladies of Charity in the United States, he established many Ladies of Charity parish chapters. In 1971, Bishop Gallagher established the Diocesan Matrimonial Tribunal.

Having been a diocesan director of youth services in the Diocese of Cleveland, 1948-61, Bishop Gallagher possessed an ability to recruit seminarians. In 1969, he was responsible for the ordination of 10 priests of the diocese: Fathers Joseph Ackerman, Melvin Bennett, Edward Dhondt, Eugene Hensell, John Lavelle, Anthony Liberatore, Joseph McCarthy, Douglas McCormack, Robert Moran, and Raymond Wieber. Altogether he ordained 66 priests for the diocese.

NEW CHALLENGES LOOM

AS the Church continued implementing the spiritual programs of Vatican II, technology affected the economy and environment. There were nuclear power plant protests and incidents in 1971 when supersonic transport was suspected of contaminating the environment. Then in 1977-1978 at Seabrook power plant and in 1979, at Three-Mile Island, there were protests against actual contaminations. A natural gas limitation in 1975 and gasoline shortage in 1979 led to the transfer or closing of automobile satellite plants from the diocese to the Sunbelt. Migrations from small town parishes began to affect parish populations. The economy experienced a recession that induced workers to emigrate from Indiana or to depend on service industry jobs operating in communities in their area.

As migration realigned Indiana's population, on January 22, 1973, the U.S. Supreme Court legalized abortion. While the United States' birth rate continued decreasing and the population grayed, the United States approached zero population growth. While both public and private schools began to consolidate or close, the nursing home industry burgeoned. In 1988, the Commission on Aging of Catholic Charities USA, which Bishop Gallagher prophetically had organized in his term as NCCC executive secretary back in 1961-1965, established the Bishop Gallagher Award for a person or group making a significant contribution to the field of aging.

In the latter 1970s, Bishop Gallagher became prominent in several other national movements. On August 15, 1976, he instituted the National Association for Pastoral Musicians and on October 2 he was elected chair of the NCCB Region VII for the Campaign for Human Development. He served as the same Region's chair from 1977-1979.

YOUTH AND LATINO OUTREACH

THE increased number of Indiana youth seeking higher education developed a need to reach out to Catholic students. At Muncie in 1972, Bishop Gallagher made the Ball State University Newman Apostolate a parish, appointing St. Mary's associate pastor Father James Bates its pastor. It is named St. Francis of Assisi Church. In 1967, a Newman Center was established at Wabash College, Crawfordsville. St. Bernard's associate pastor Father Kenneth Raczek had begun a Newman Club there in 1960; Bishop Gallagher appointed a subsequent St. Bernard's associate pastor, Father Frederick Hofheinz, Newman Center chaplain. This Newman Center closed in 2002, then in 2003 reopened in its original association with St. Bernard Church.

In addition, after the United States' 1975 withdrawal from the Vietnam conflict, Asian Pacific immigrants swelled, and a new influx of Latin Americans began moving north, rousing the Church to cultural conflicts that it thought were past history. Especially the Latino Americans challenged Church ministry since their Catholicism predates the United States where the Church has changed. A gallant effort was made to minister to a growing Hispanic population at Marion when St. Paul Church relocated from its downtown Branson Street site to its suburban site on Kem Road. In 1976, Bishop Gallagher

◆ Bishop Fulcher

arranged for St. Paul's former church to be Our Lady of Guadalupe mission with Father Frederick Perry, a former missionary in the Society of St. James, developing it. In 1991, Bishop William Higi made it a Latino parish with Father Peter Vanderkolk as pastor. It continued until 1994.

Missions became parishes and other parishes, established during Bishop Gallagher's time, include St. Alphonsus, Zionsville, 1972; St. Cecilia, DeMotte, 1974; St. Louis de Montfort, Fishers, 1978; and St. Elizabeth Ann Seton, Carmel, 1981.

Upon Msgr. Schall's 1970 retirement, Bishop Gallagher named Msgr. Emil Schweier his vicar general, 1970-79, and then Msgr. William Higi, 1979-82.

BISHOP FULCHER SUCCEEDS BISHOP GALLAGHER

THOUGH burdened with diabetes and phlebitis, Bishop Gallagher maintained a regular sched-ule. On October 26, 1982, he retired and was named apostolic administrator of the diocese until his successor's

◆ Billboard welcoming
Bishop Fulcher

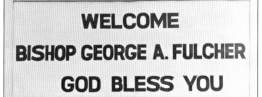

WELCOME
BISHOP GEORGE A. FULCHER
GOD BLESS YOU

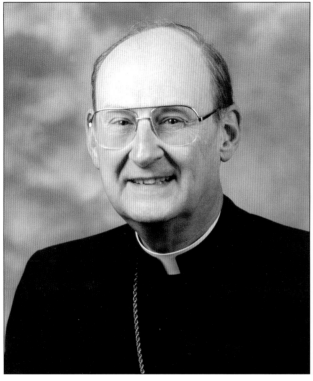

Bishop Higi

Outreach to Haiti from Our Lady of Mt. Carmel

he was appointed Bishop Gallagher's vicar general in 1979 and Bishop Fulcher's in 1983. His own vicars general have been Msgr. John Duncan, 1984-1991, and Msgr. Robert Sell since 1991.

the wheel, the Parke County coroner ruled that Bishop Fulcher "died of smoke inhalation and injuries received in the auto accident, as well as injuries he received in the fire that followed." His flipped car exploded in flames. After his funeral on February 1 at the Cathedral of St. Mary of the Immaculate Conception, his body was buried in St. Mary Cemetery, Lafayette.

The diocesan chancellor, Msgr. William Higi, 51, had been elected diocesan administrator on January 26. In April it was announced that Pope John Paul II had appointed Msgr. Higi the fifth Bishop of Lafayette-in-Indiana. Archbishop Edward O'Meara of Indianapolis ordained him a bishop and installed him in the Lafayette cathedral on June 6, 1984. A native of Anderson, Bishop Higi studied for the priesthood at Mount St. Mary of the West, Cincinnati, where he also received a master's degree from Xavier University. Bishop John Carberry had ordained him a priest at Lafayette on May 30, 1959. After various pastoral assignments, particularly at Lake Village, 1970-1984, and with Lafayette chancery service since 1962,

Bishop Higi visits Haiti

OUTREACH TO HAITI

THE diocese's Haiti outreach began in the 1980s. By 1989, Bishop Higi made it diocesan policy to be active in social and humanitarian outreach by encouraging parishes to establish ties with other parishes "and in a special way with a parish in Haiti." The diocese itself, in cooperation with the Sisters of St. Joseph of Tipton, provides funding for a multi-purpose mission called Hospice St. Joseph in Port-au-Prince. In 1996 and again in 1999, Bishop Higi visited Hospice St. Joseph. Fourteen parishes have twinned with Haitian parishes. Three other parishes and one institution contribute directly to Hospice St. Joseph. Other parishes implement the policy by twinning with and supporting outreach to Central and South American, European, African, Middle Eastern or United States missions.

PASTORAL PLANNING

ONE of Bishop Higi's first challenges was to develop a planning task force that Bishop Fulcher had begun in January 1984. Task force members were Fathers Louis Heitz, chair, Melvin Bennett, Richard DiGeronimo, Douglas McCormack and John Zahn; Sister Eugenia Latendresse, CSJ, Sister Mary

St. Maria Goretti Church dedication, 2004

Three Lafayette bishops, 1984

Dianne, SND, Mr. Raymond Rufo, and Mr. James Savage. The task force was to "assess existing conditions and needs of diocesan instrumentalities partially or fully funded by the Diocese of Lafayette-in-Indiana." The group issued reports on August 28, 1984, and January 7, 1985.

The Lilly Foundation offered a grant to hold a diocesan convocation to develop a pastoral planning process. A convocation of clergy was held in 1986 at the French Lick Springs Hotel where a diocesan pastoral plan was instigated and subsequently promulgated in 1988 for deanery and parish implementation. The plan was reviewed and revised annually through 1999. In 2000, after a yearlong planning process, Bishop Higi promulgated the "Crossroads" pastoral plan and invited nominees for membership on its implementation committee.

The 2000 plan's four goals were to provide quality

Catholic education and formation for children, youth, and adults in the Gospel's service; to strengthen and expand leadership competencies in the diocese; to call the people of the Local Church to a deeper union with God; and to call the people of the Local Church to evangelize their own faith communities, especially youth, young adults, Hispanic and the inactive and alienated.

Pastoral planning in recent years has focused on future parish staffing and parish clustering.

DEMOGRAPHICS AND DEANERIES

BELOW is a table of the diocese's deanery populations from the 1990 and 2000 U.S. censuses comparing civil and Catholic numbers:

	Civilian 1990	Catholic 1990	Civilian 2000	Catholic 2000	Catholic 2005
Anderson Deanery	220,957	12,147	223,338	10,293	8,839
Carmel Deanery	147,083	18,435	228,847	36,619	43,730
Fowler Deanery	47,952	7,883	54,030	8,830	7,077
Lafayette Deanery	221,992	16,654	246,823	17,620	18,497
Logansport Deanery	148,867	10,824	241,674	15,580	15,199
Muncie Deanery	182,386	9,383	182,024	8,451	7,243
Totals		75,326		97,393	100,585

The chart shows that while suburban migration to the diocese's northern counties in the Fowler, Monticello, and Logansport deaneries stabilized in the 1990s, the migration to Boone, Hamilton, and south Madison counties in the Lafayette and Anderson deaneries continued unabated. In 1990 the Carmel Deanery, consisting of Boone and Hamilton counties, was created, replacing the Monticello Deanery, which was dissolved and its counties returned to their former deaneries. In 1991, Holy Spirit Parish, Fishers, and in 1995, St. Maria Goretti Parish, Westfield, were established. On June 26, 2005, another new parish was begun in Fall Creek Township, Hamilton County: St. John Vianney Parish, Fishers.

These developments reflect the diocese's continued suburbanization, a process that has been part of its history from the start of the industrial age at the turn of the last century. Because of this process, the Pulaski and Cicero parishes were consolidated about 1900. The Gas Boom parish at Gas City was rebuilt and renamed. Countryside churches moved into towns: Harrison to Lucerne; Grass Creek to Kewanna; St. Anthony's, Dehners Corner, to Goodland, Earl Park, Kentland or Fowler. Rochester's church on the town's outskirts moved into Rochester, and Barrydale combined with Otterbein. In Lafayette, St. Ann's chapel became a parish in 1884, while St. Lawrence Parish was established in 1895 in the city's Linnwood annex. Parishes relocated to developing sections of their respective cities in West Lafayette, 1958; Crawfordsville, 1958; Frankfort, 1968; Marion, 1977; Noblesville, 1991; and St. Joan of Arc, Kokomo, 2004. The Logansport parishes of St. Vincent de Paul, St. Joseph, and St. Bridget, all of which were established in mission days, were consolidated in 1985 into All Saints to strengthen the Church's unity and her evangelization mission. Every other parish in the diocese has experienced replacement at its site or contemporary renovations. The Cathedral of St. Mary of the Immaculate Conception was extensively renovated and rededicated in 2001.

◆ *Blessed Theodore Guerin High School, Noblesville*

The 2000 Glenmary Research Center lists Benton, Hamilton, Pulaski, Jasper and Tippecanoe counties with the highest percentage of Catholics, and Clinton, Carroll, Randolph and Warren counties with the lowest. Delaware County, at 72 percent, is the diocese's highest unchurched county; Benton County, at 33.1 percent, is the lowest unchurched county. This means that in one county 72 percent of the people claim no church, in the other 33.1 percent make such a claim. In both these counties the most people attending any church are Catholic, that is, 21.8 percent in Delaware County and 51.8 percent in Benton County.

ACTIVATING MINISTRIES

PROFESSIONALIZING the Local Church's ministries became a hallmark of Bishop Higi's service. This was accomplished not only in the 1985 opening of the Catholic Pastoral Center, Lafayette, where diocesan offices were relocated, but also in the implementation of professional financial accounting standards and in the development of adult education programs. The Fruitful Harvest Campaign has been held every other year since 1984, replacing traditional annual assessments on parish offertory income – a practice of fewer than 15 U.S. dioceses. The Catholic Foundation for Northcentral Indiana was organized in 1997 and is overseen by a Pastoral Office for Stewardship and Development, which also coordinates fund raising and planned giving efforts in the context of Christian stewardship.

The Ecclesial Lay Ministry program, proposed in the 1994 pastoral plan, is associated with Saint Joseph's College, Rensselaer. It provides accredited diocesan-wide adult education and formation programs suited to persons pursuing Church ministries. Furthering Catholic school education, junior high grades were added to Lafayette Central Catholic High School in 1996. In the last 20 years, parochial schools have opened at St. Maria Goretti, Westfield; Our Lady of Grace, Noblesville; St. Louis de Montfort, Fishers; and St. Bernard, Crawfordsville. In August 2004, Bishop Higi dedicated Blessed Theodore Guerin High School, Noblesville.

PASTORAL OFFICES

THE Pastoral Office for Formation includes youth and parish religious education, worship and liturgy departments and a resource center. The Indiana Catholic Conference representative functions from the Pastoral Office for Planning and Communications. The Pastoral Office for Administration coordinates financial services and Fruitful Harvest collections.

◈ *Sisters of St. Francis anniversary celebration, 2000*

Besides maintaining canonical consultative bodies such as the presbyteral council, finance council, priestly life and ministry department, and personnel board, the diocese has colleges of consultors and of deans, a vocations director, and a permanent diaconate vicar. The first class of diocesan-sponsored permanent deacons was ordained in 2005, although permanent deacons ordained elsewhere have served in parishes for 20 years. In 2002, Bishop Higi encouraged the founding of the Notre Dame Sisters of the Eucharistic Heart at Lafayette. When it did not succeed, one Sister took up residence at the Sisters Adorers of the Precious Blood Monastery to engage in ministry to the elderly until her departure in 2005. The other formed the Notre Dame Sisters of Joyful Hope serving at St. Joan of Arc, Kokomo.

The diocese's judicial vicar oversees its tribunal, and a superintendent maintains the Pastoral Office for Catholic Schools. There are 22 Catholic schools in the diocese. An ecumenical officer and the Propagation of the Faith director promote outreach to other Christians and spreading the Gospel in mission lands. In response to contemporary social circumstances, the diocese maintains an Assistance Ministry for abuse concerns.

WORKS OF CHARITY

MANY of the hospitals and health care facilities that were begun as ministries of charity in the late 19th and early 20th centuries remain viable today. The Sisters of St. Francis Seraph of Perpetual Adoration have operated St. Elizabeth Hospital, Lafayette, from 1876 to the present. They also ran St. Joseph Hospital, Logansport, 1893-1974; and St. Anthony Home for the Aged, Lafayette, 1897-1960. The Sisters of St. Joseph of Tipton opened Good Samaritan Home, Kokomo, 1921-1970; Villa Maria Nursing Home, 1948-1968; and Mercy Hospital, Elwood, 1926. The Sisters of the Holy Cross opened St. John's Hickey Memorial

◈ *Bishop Higi with children at Bryant*

Hospital, Anderson, 1910. Sisters of St. Francis of Maryville, Missouri, conducted St. Ann's Hospital, Peru, 1906-1924.

In the United States during the 1990s, health care developed into a significant industry. The Sisters of St. Francis Seraph of Perpetual Adoration consolidated St. Elizabeth Hospital with Lafayette's Home Hospital, and, as Greater Lafayette Health Services, are the third largest employer in Tippecanoe County. The Daughters of Charity, Indianapolis, met the challenge from their St. Vincent Hospital system that either built extensions or took possession of hospitals at Anderson, Carmel, Elwood, Frankfort, Kokomo, Winchester and Williamsport.

While parishes have been challenged to minister to parishioners in local health care facilities, Lafayette Catholics opened and continue to administer St. Anthony Health Care. The Franciscan Sisters of Chicago Service Corporation took possession of or built George Davis Manor, West Lafayette; St. Mary Healthcare, Lafayette; St. Elizabeth Healthcare, Delphi; and University Place, West Lafayette. St. Elizabeth Hospital, Lafayette, instituted St. Elizabeth Hospice. The Anderson parishes of St. Mary and St. Ambrose participate in United Faith Housing Corporation that maintains three senior citizen housing

◆ *Bishop Higi with Cardinal Carberry, 1995*

facilities. St. Joseph Center, Tipton, has renovated former convent space into senior housing units.

The former Catholic Charities was transferred in 1985 to a Pastoral Office for Social Ministry, reflecting a birthrate decline that made child placement services no longer feasible. Subsequently, diocesan family life ministries have sponsored ongoing Natural Family Planning programs; ministries to divorced, separated, and remarried Catholics; Project Rachel; Rachel's Vineyard; and Project Gianna.

LATINO MINISTRY

SINCE 1952, the diocese has ministered to migrant workers who come to North Central Indiana annually to harvest truck crops. In recent decades, the cooperation of the Society of Our Lady of the Most Holy Trinity from Texas has made interaction between the workers and local parishes more effective. From St. Mary, Alexandria, and St. Joseph, Elwood, or St. Joan of Arc, Kokomo, Masses are held at camps during harvest season. At season's end, a gathering with the bishop administering confirmation and first Holy Communion is held at one of the area parishes.

In the 1990s, Indiana's Hispanic migration echoed the national trend of a great influx of Central and South American Latinos. This has brought about a Hispanic Ministry department. Regular Masses in Spanish are now celebrated in parishes across the diocese, including St. Boniface, Lafayette (designated the city's Hispanic center); United Methodist Church, Akron; St. Mary, Anderson;

Our Lady of Mt. Carmel, Carmel; St. Patrick, Kokomo; St. Joseph, Delphi; St. Mary, Frankfort; St. Joan of Arc, Kokomo; St. Bernard, Crawfordsville; All Saints, Logansport; St. Paul, Marion; Our Lady of the Lakes, Monticello; St. Lawrence, Muncie; Our Lady of Grace, Noblesville; Immaculate Conception, Portland; St. Augustine, Rensselaer; and St. Mary, Union City. Bishop Higi has appointed a vicar for Hispanics in White County and surrounding areas at Monticello.

EUCHARISTIC ADORATION

ON November 14, 1994, Bishop Higi wrote a column in The Catholic Moment on American culture and Catholicism. The column reviews the long journey of the Catholic faith in the United States reflected in the diocese's history. Its fundamental question is: Will the Catholics of the United States remain faithful to the countercultural values of their faith, or will ever-increasing numbers succumb to secularization? The answer is being given in greater expressions of faith, especially in increased Eucharistic adoration.

Not only have parishes added occasions of adoration of Jesus in the Blessed Sacrament, but perpetual adoration chapels have opened at St. Louis de Montfort, Fishers, in 1995; St. Elizabeth Medical Center, Lafayette, in 1997; Our Lady of Mt. Carmel, in 2002; and St. Patrick, Kokomo, in 2003. Bishop Higi has promoted beseeching Jesus in the Blessed Sacrament for an increase in vocations to the diocesan priesthood. During the 1994 diocesan jubilee, The Catholic Moment editor Thomas Russell observed that Bishop Higi accentuates the diocese's history-in-the-making, not in terms of its achievements, but in Christ.

◆ *Bishop Higi with Pope John Paul II*

◈ Bishop Higi with Indiana's Bishop Melczek, Bishop Gettelfinger, Bishop D'Arcy and Archbishop Buechlein

◈ Jubilee Year 2000

NEW EVANGELIZATION

SECULARIZATION has produced statistics that other churches are continuing to lose membership, but that the Catholic Church is growing. The 2000 Glenmary Research Center reveals that Catholics are now the majority religion even in the most unchurched counties of the diocese. Benton, Boone, Cass, Delaware, Hamilton, Howard, Jasper, Jay, Newton, Pulaski, Tippecanoe and Tipton counties all have Catholics now as the highest total church adherents. Blackford, Fulton, Miami and White counties have a second most; Clinton, Grant, Madison, Montgomery, Randolph and Fountain have the third most; and Warren and Carroll, the fourth most. These are all high ranks, considering the many denominations represented.

◈ Year of the Eucharist, October 2004-October 2005

Even in the most unchurched counties of the diocese, Catholics are a majority among churchgoers. Catholics may be a minority in their counties' total civilian populations, but they are the strongest churches in more than half the counties of the diocese.

The same statistics reveal decreases in vocations to the priesthood. In 2004, the diocese welcomed the services of three priests from the Diocese of Orlu, Nigeria, and in 2005, one from the Archdiocese of San Jose, Costa Rica. On September 13, 2005, Bishop Higi held a clergy conference at Frankfort to motivate leadership for parishes under 500 households to cluster their resources not only to share the limited priestly ministry available, but also to strengthen the Church's evangelization base.

At the 60th anniversary celebration of the diocese, Bishop Higi prayed to the Lord of the harvest to send laborers to his vineyard (Matt. 9:38). But since the days of Bishop Simon Bruté, who began with only three priests, the laborers have always been few. Bishops, priests, religious and faithful have communicated the Catholic faith across the decades of the Diocese of Lafayette and the centuries preceding, in a land hungering for the message of the Church. Perhaps it began from the banks of the Wabash River when the first Catholic made the Sign of the Cross from a canoe at Ouiatanon in 1717. A wondering native may have asked, "Could you tell me the meaning of that Sign?" From the scattered Catholics who migrated from parishes in Quebec, Baltimore and Bardstown, the Diocese of Lafayette-in-Indiana grew from the Vincennes and Fort Wayne dioceses to 31,700 Catholics at the founding of the diocese in 1945; to 83,603 in 1970; to 91,526 in 1995; and to 100,585 in 2005. As Bishop Higi says, "Praised be Jesus Christ!" And his flock, confirmed in the faith of its forbearers, resoundingly responds: "Now and forever!"

◈ *Cathedral of St. Mary of the Immaculate Conception*

PART TWO

Parishes

of the

Diocese

of

Lafayette-in-Indiana

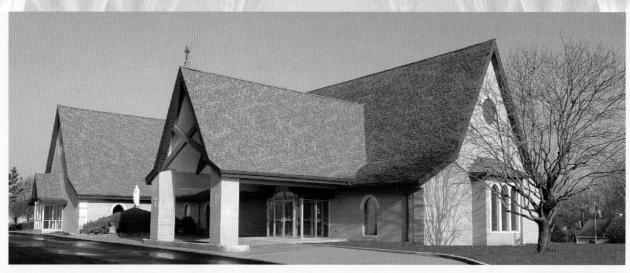

◆ *St. Mary Church*

ST. MARY ◆ ALEXANDRIA

THE fund drive initiated by Father Thomas Zimmer (1963-1970) in 1963 brought in sufficient capital to build the present St. Mary Church in Alexandria, which Bishop Raymond Gallagher dedicated on April 2, 1963. The town, which goes back to 1840, still had only eight Irish Catholic families in 1870. With the growth of the 1890 Gas Boom era, priests from Elwood held Masses in a log cabin, people's homes and a local hall. In 1896, Bishop Joseph Rademacher appointed Father Joachim Baker Alexandria's first resident pastor. He built the 1897 church on the town's west side. The School Sisters of Notre Dame staffed the parochial school on the church's first floor.

School enrollment rose and fell with the town's economic fortunes, but in 1930 an addition was made. Father Leo Scheetz (1931-1949) moved the church downstairs. The School Sisters resided in the church-school building until 1954 when Father Robert Sorg built a convent. The nearly century-old school building was demolished in 1987 to be replaced with a modern facility while Father Philip Haslinger (1985-1999) served at St. Mary's. At the school's 1997 centennial, ground was broken for a 19,000 square foot Haslinger Family Life Center, now containing a gymnasium-auditorium with stage and a school kitchen, extra classrooms, a weight room and a walking track. The School Sisters still maintain a presence at St. Mary's School, kindergarten through eighth grade.

Regular ground improvements have resulted in decorative plantings, an updated grotto and a modern playground. Under direction of current pastor, Father Paul Cochran, a complete renovation of the church exterior and interior was completed in 2006. In 2005, the parish was clustered with St. Joseph, Elwood.

◆ *First church and school building, 1897*

◆ *Groundbreaking for Haslinger Family Center, 1997*

◆ *St. Ambrose Church*

ST. AMBROSE ◆ ANDERSON

BISHOP JOHN CARBERRY dedicated St. Ambrose Church on December 16, 1962. Bishop John Bennett had established the parish on July 2, 1947, with Father Francis Kienly as pastor. On October 12, 1948, Father Fred Potthoff became the pastor. That fall, a school and chapel (the present school building) were erected for use until the church basement was dedicated on August 1, 1954. The former chapel became additional classrooms and meeting space. In 1960, parishioners remodeled the church basement into the Ambrosian Hall.

On September 15, 1950, Holy Cross Sisters opened the parochial school, staying until 1974. Adding a kindergarten, the school resumed under a lay faculty. In 1987, St. Ambrose School was the first in Madison County to inaugurate a full-day kindergarten and shortly thereafter

introduced a pre-school in The Early Childhood Center. Under Father Charles Kline (1978-84), an elected parish board of education was formed in 1980. In 1986, Father Edward Dhondt reorganized the parish council.

Under Father Thomas Heilman in 1958, a Men's Choir became active and the Confraternity of Christian Doctrine was formed to instruct public school children. The School Bus Association was supported by weekly bingo, proceeds of which went to purchase new buses, until 1983. During the 1980s, St. Ambrose School Parents Club was formed and religious education and liturgy directors were hired. In 1997, the parish introduced a Special Religious Education program for disabled children. Monthly Eucharistic Exposition and Adoration was also begun that year.

St. Ambrose supported Hospice St. Joseph in Port-au-Prince, Haiti, and then transferred its support to the Haiti Medical Mission Team and their annual ministry to the Petit Trous de Nippes parish there. St. Mary and St. Ambrose parishioners have also been involved in a Catholic Bible Study at Correctional Industrial Facility, Pendleton.

◆ *St. Ambrose School student body, 2000*

◆ *Father Dhondt after the Easter Vigil*

ST. MARY ✦ ANDERSON

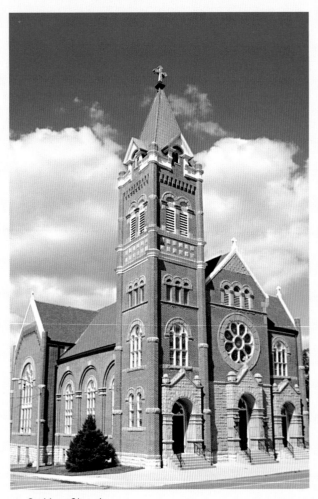

◆ *St. Mary Church*

(1955-1976) closed the high school in 1966 when the Holy Cross Sisters departed.

One way to raise funds in the 19th century was to rent pews. At the pews' auction, the north end Irish were the only high bidders for the first 10 pews, and the south end Dutch, as Germans were called in those days, took the next 10. For several years, at the Sunday collection the priest followed the altar server and recorded what each gave. This brought on a petition to transfer Father Mulcahy. But Joseph Abel's parish history says it did no good because he was a fighting Irishman, too, though Scottish born Father Mulcahy was reared in Cleveland, Ohio.

After Father Thomas Mongovan's service (1911-1917), Msgr. Travers served in Anderson from 1917-1955. He is remembered as St. Mary's most beloved pastor. St. Mary's pastor since 1984 is Father Robert Williams.

◆ *St. Mary addition, built in 1964*

BISHOP JOSEPH RADEMACHER dedicated Anderson's third St. Mary's Church on October 6, 1895. The first church, whose foundation Father Michael Clarke from Lafayette had laid in 1858, was removed and St. Mary's third cornerstone was laid on July 9, 1894. Logansport missionaries had ministered to Irish canal and railroad workers in various sites until Father John McMahon from Union City (1862-1867) built Anderson's first church on Father Clarke's foundation. Father John Crawley (1866-1884), also from Union City, laid a cornerstone for a second church on July 4, 1875, and built a one-story frame rectory, which was replaced with Father Frederick Weichmann's Victorian rectory, 1884-1891.

Lay teachers taught St. Mary's parochial school from 1869 until the Holy Cross Sisters came in 1879. By 1898, Father Dennis Mulcahy converted the second church into a school and sisters' residence. In 1920, Father Thomas Travers began a new school building and opened a complete high school. Msgr. Francis Kienly

◆ *Holy Cross Sister in typing class*

ST. JOSEPH ◆ ELWOOD

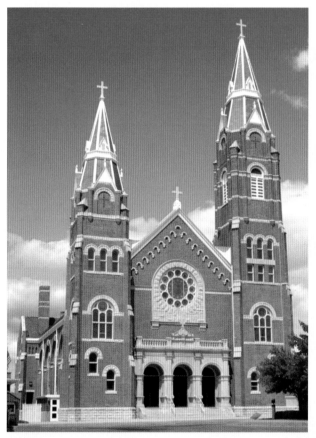

◆ *St. Joseph Church*

cornerstone on October 8, 1899. The upper church was completed in 1901.

Father Theodore Hammes, the first director of the Diocesan Thanksgiving clothing drive, served this parish from 1941-1967. Upon his retirement, Msgr. Hammes lived to be 100 years old. He was interred in St. Joseph Cemetery.

St. Joseph School, established in 1891, was taught by Sisters of St. Joseph of Tipton from 1894 to 1970. After it was fire-damaged in 1894 and repaired with a second story, it was replaced in 1939 with a large brick, two-story structure razed in 1977 to make space for the parish multi-purpose center. Bishop Raymond Gallagher dedicated St. Joseph Multi-purpose Center on November 2, 1980. It consists of the Biegel meeting rooms and four religious education classrooms on the lower level; on the ground floor are the Heitz Library and Reardon Hall, equipped with a kitchen and storage room.

In 1925, St. Joseph Parish conveyed two city lots to the Sisters of St. Joseph of Tipton to open Mercy Hospital, now St. Vincent Mercy Hospital. Since 2005, St. Joseph has been clustered with St. Mary, Alexandria. In 2005, St. Joseph's 404 households consisted of 1,014 persons.

BISHOP JOSEPH DWENGER established St. Joseph Parish on June 15, 1889. He sent Father Balthasar Biegel to Elwood on July 28 to transform its mission once served at irregular intervals from the 1850s by Fathers Daniel Molony of Indianapolis, Michael Clarke of Lafayette and John Crawley and Frederick Weichmann of Anderson. Msgr. Biegel remained at St. Joseph until his death on August 12, 1935. With impetus from the 1897 gas boom, the mission church for 175 people grew into a parish of 1,400. Fort Wayne diocesan administrator Father John Guendling laid its

◆ *Mercy Hospital in Elwood*

◆ *Cemetery at St. Joseph Parish*

HOLY FAMILY ◆ GAS CITY

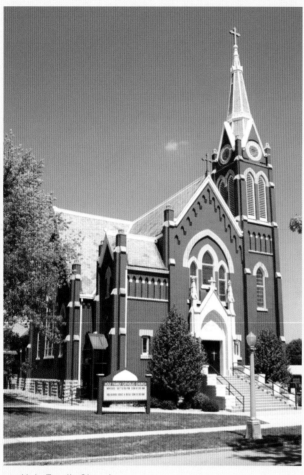

◆ Holy Family Church

BISHOP HERMAN ALERDING dedicated Holy Family Church on October 2, 1910. This parish's story began when Father Frederick Weichmann was commissioned to start a Catholic church in Harrisburg, as Gas City was known before the 1897 gas boom. The first Mass was celebrated in the U.S. Glass barracks in 1892. The following year the Gas City Land Company donated seven lots on North A Street, making it possible for St. Genevieve Church to be erected there that year.

The brick Victorian rectory built in 1894 is still in use after many renovations. Father Weichmann dreamed of a new and larger brick church on the property's corner, but died in 1905 before it could be realized. In 1906, his successor Father Charles McCabe made his dream a reality. The new church was named Holy Family.

At first most of the parish men were bottle blowers or associated with glass and bottle companies fired by the industry. A 1995 parish history credits the parish women with erasing the parish debt through dinners and various fundraisers. Irish, German, and Belgian families constituted the parish in early years. Though much changed over the years, Holy Family remains and has adapted to the times.

The church's most beautiful features are its windows. The stained- and painted-glass windows were made in Germany. They have been conscientiously cleaned, repaired and maintained. Visitors still comment on their traditional beauty.

Since Father Weichmann also cared for the nearby Soldiers' Home, the U.S. government built a Gothic Chapel of St. Ignatius Loyola there in 1899. It has since become part of the Veterans Administration Northern Indiana Health Care System. Though it has had various chaplains since its inauguration, Holy Family's priests have continued to provide its religious services.

◆ Dedication 1910

ST. PAUL ◆ MARION

BISHOP RAYMOND GALLAGHER dedicated the third St. Paul Church on May 8, 1977. Plans had been approved on March 24, 1974, to relocate the parish from its South Branson Street site to Kem Road where St. Paul's elementary and high school had been combined in 1973. Groundbreaking was held on May 23, 1976. Soon afterwards a new rectory was built on its south side.

In July 1868, Father B. Theodore Borg of Peru celebrated Marion's first Mass in a wooden frame church at 9th and Branson Streets. Father Bernard Kroeger, also from Peru, who had been saying monthly Masses around town since 1865, bought the lots for the frame church. With Father Patrick Frawley's arrival in 1875, a new rectory went up. In time, ground was broken for a Gothic church designed by Marion architect Bert L. French. The cornerstone was laid on May 7, 1896. On November 7, 1897, Bishop Joseph Rademacher dedicated the 900-seating capacity church in honor of the Conversion of St. Paul.

Marion's population after World War II tripled. St. Paul parochial school began in the new church basement in 1909, the Sisters of St. Joseph of Tipton staffing it. In 1910, a large, red brick school building was built on the first church's site. By 1924, enrollment from the first to the tenth grade rose to 217. Its first

◆ *Branson Street St. Paul's sanctuary, 1937*

high school class graduated in 1933. In September 1951, Bishop John Bennett dedicated a new, 16-bedroom convent. The following year a building fund drive to renovate the school structures developed to a revision that eventually built St. Paul's Bennett High School on Kem Road. Its first class graduated in 1956.

St. Paul's preschool through sixth grade currently has 120 pupils. The parish with its present pastor, Father Richard Weisenberger, serves approximately 900 households.

◆ *St. Paul Church*

ST. JOHN THE BAPTIST
◆ TIPTON

◆ *Choir view, 2004*

◆ *St. John the Baptist Church*

Bishop William Higi rededicated the renovated St. John the Baptist Church on June 24, 2004. A 2003 lightning strike at the church tower caused fire and smoke damage that brought about a complete renovation. While Father Leroy Kinnaman has been its pastor since 2000, the 450 seating capacity church accommodates 395 households of 945 persons.

Tipton's second church had been dedicated on Aug. 30, 1891. Earlier missionaries from Lafayette, Peru, and Kokomo had visited here until Father Bernard Kroeger with Bishop John Luers' permission obtained lots in 1866. In 1875, Father Francis Lordemann from Kokomo built a frame church for 15 households so in July 1876 Bishop Joseph Dwenger sent Father Francis Lentz as Tipton's first resident pastor. But due to a defective fireplace flue, this church burned down on Dec. 14, 1885.

In 1889, the new brick church's cornerstone was laid. At Father Anthony Kroeger's arrival in 1890, the church and a brick convent were completed for its 1891

dedication. The present convent was built in 1961. The church's towers were finished in 1898. He added its stained glass windows in 1903 prior to its 1904 redecoration.

A two-story school and social hall had been built in 1885. It was staffed by laity till 1888 when the Sisters of St. Joseph began teaching there. Father Kroeger assisted these Sisters who resided in a cottage until an 1891 convent was built to obtain property for a motherhouse north of town.

Between 1914-20, Father Joseph Bilstein oversaw the shamrock stone work covering the church exterior and installed its present three bells. Father Jerome Walski laid the new school's cornerstone in 1950. He redecorated the church in 1955, as did Father John Bouvier in 1982. Father Fred Gschwind, 1987-2000, purchased additional church property and restored its present stained glass windows.

◆ *Ravages of fire, 2003*

OUR LADY OF MT. CARMEL
◆ CARMEL

◆ *Bishop breaks ground for church addition, 2001*

Our Lady of Mt. Carmel has experienced much growth in parish education ministries from youth to adult. At a 2001 groundbreaking, another expansion program created meeting space for adult education programs, a perpetual adoration chapel, the Hall of American Saints, additional seating in the church proper, an elevator and more accessible worship space.

The parish has also established a Hispanic Apostolate in which more than 170 families participate in various programs. The Matthew 25 Center and the Trinity Free Clinic serve the poor in Hamilton County. Parishioners maintain a relationship with a sister parish of St. Antoine-de-Padoue, Petite Riviere, Haiti.

As a parish served by Father Richard Doerr as pastor since 2004, Our Lady of Mt. Carmel is grateful for all who built, contributed to, and continue to maintain its strong spiritual and loving family.

BISHOP JOHN BENNETT established Our Lady of Mt. Carmel Parish in 1955. Father M. Joseph McDonnell (1955-69) celebrated its first Mass for 60 families at the old Carmel Theatre. By September 16, 1956, the parish of 163 families built a rectory, a convent, and an eight-classroom structure used as a church, which Coadjutor Bishop John Carberry dedicated. After the leadership of Father Fred Gschwind (1969-1972,) Father W. Michael Kettron (1972-1987) witnessed Bishop Raymond Gallagher dedicate a larger church on July 16, 1975, to accommodate the increased Catholic population, which by 1980 grew to 1,500 families. In 1978, St. Louis de Montfort Parish, Fishers, and in 1981, St. Elizabeth Ann Seton Parish, Carmel, were developed out of Our Lady of Mt. Carmel. During Monsignor John Duncan's pastorate (1987-2004), St. Maria Goretti Parish, Westfield, was developed in 1995, first with a school and then a church that Bishop William Higi dedicated on Dec. 8, 2004.

◆ *Aerial view, 1972*

◆ *Our Lady of Mt. Carmel Church*

ST. ELIZABETH ANN SETON
◆ CARMEL

◆ *Groundbreaking ceremony for church, 1983*

◆ *Construction of parish life center in progress, 2005*

Bishop Raymond Gallagher established St. Elizabeth Ann Seton Parish on July 1, 1981, to serve Catholics in Clay and Washington townships, Hamilton County. The initial 250 households that gathered at Woodbrook Elementary School ("St. Woodbrook") increased to 880 by the time Father Leo Piguet (1981-1998) had Bishop William Higi dedicate its new church on October 20, 1985. The Alwine White Pennsylvania brick and glass main building accommodates 900 people, its unique design meriting an award from the North American Liturgical Conference. The church's only addition has been a striking crucifix by St. Louis sculptor Wiktor Szostalo that Father Theodore Rothrock had hung at the front of its worship space in 2003. From its 234 households in 1981, St. Elizabeth Ann Seton Parish grew to 1,900 households by the turn of the century.

Fifty distinct parish ministries from athletics to welcoming serve the parish of more than 2,000 registered households. Active ministries include evangelization, parish council, peace and justice, Christ Renews His Parish, religious education formation for children to adults, sacramental preparation and growing devotion to the Blessed Sacrament. Under Father Rothrock's leadership, the Knights of Columbus initiated a 1999 Bishop Fulcher Chapter. On a continual basis, St. Elizabeth Ann Seton supports its sister parish, St. Genevieve in Haiti, with spiritual and medical missions. As a tithing parish, the church donates a tenth of weekly offering to a selected organization. Community social and spiritual outreach programs have fostered its reputation as the "most welcoming parish."

Having expanded its physical layout in 2002 and built a new rectory in 2003, St. Elizabeth Ann Seton broke ground for a Parish Life Center to accommodate growing religious formation classes and offer a multipurpose educational and recreational environment for the entire community. It also houses a newly initiated parish pre-school, which opened in late 2005.

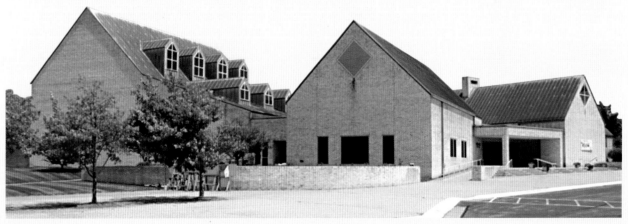

◆ *St. Elizabeth Ann Seton Church*

SACRED HEART OF JESUS
◆ CICERO

Bishop Raymond Gallagher appointed Father Duane Craycraft Cicero's first resident pastor of Sacred Heart of Jesus Parish on July 1, 1978. From 1972 it had been Father Craycraft's mission from Tipton. The DeMontfort Missionaries from Noblesville served there from 1944 to 1948. The same priest came weekly from 1948 to 1963 when the only priest at Noblesville cared for both congregations until 1972. From 1927 to 1944, the Redemptorists from Lebanon served the mission and from 1912 to 1927, Tipton chaplains.

◆ *Original church building*

In 1900, the Cicero mission consolidated Hamilton County's mission churches opened in 1864: St. Mary, Buscher's Settlement, and St. John, Mullin's Settlement. During the gas boom, Bishop Joseph Rademacher acceded to the Washington Glass Company's petition for a church for its Catholic employees. Elwood's pastor Father Balthasar Biegel was sent to arrange this in Hamilton County. Bishop Rademacher missioned Frankfort's pastor Father Peter O'Reilly to care for Cicero and the Noblesville mission of St. Vincent de Paul (1899-1906). Sacred Heart Church, built in 1900, was first used on January 30, 1901. Bishop Herman Alerding dedicated it that year on September 29. Noblesville Catholics took the interurban to worship there. Frankfort's pastor cared for the mission until the Tipton chaplains were assigned in 1912.

Father Craycraft purchased Sacred Heart's present rectory in 1975, St. Anne's religious education building in 1976 and St. Mark's pre-school in 1983. Father Gerald Borawski was pastor from 1984 to 1987. Since Father Michael Kettron's arrival in 1989, a parish hall was created in the church basement. A St. Francis parish business office was purchased in 1991 and in 1992, the yellow brick property. On February 21, 1998, Bishop William Higi dedicated a new religious education center and the renovated basement social hall to serve 210 households. At present 167 households comprise Sacred Heart of Jesus Parish.

◆ *Sacred Heart of Jesus Church*

HOLY SPIRIT ◆ FISHERS

◆ Dedication Mass, 1994

◆ Groundbreaking ceremony for church, 1993

Bishop William Higi dedicated Holy Spirit Church at Geist on October 9, 1994. The Fall Creek township parish opened in July 1990 at a strip mall storefront on 96th Street. On September 10, people participated in its first Mass at Fall Creek Elementary School gymnasium. When Bishop Higi approved the parish name in October, it ratified the parish's first campaign theme: "Catch the Spirit" was both appropriate and prophetic. By December, religious education classes began and at Christmas the gymnasium was filled to capacity.

At the time Bishop Higi presided at the March 1993 church groundbreaking, Holy Spirit had engaged 100 parishioners in Mass ministries, enrolled 71 adult participants in RENEW and Bible study programs and involved 15 parish sponsors and candidates in its RCIA program. Fourteen instructors and 11 aides in 12 homes taught 147 youth in religious education classes. Outreach programs held food/clothing drives for the needy.

A budget and fiscal projections for parish development were prepared. The parish held three parish wide social events and served 7,200 doughnut holes after Sunday Masses.

The 34,000-square-foot church seats 900 people and includes a chapel, a social hall with a commercial kitchen, a library, an education wing with 13 classrooms and a suite of administrative and religious education offices. Spirited services from the gymnasium moved to the church on August 13, 1994. With community outreach as a priority since 1994, Holy Spirit parishioners have provided toys and money for Dayspring Homeless Shelter. Parish volunteers transported more than 250 cases of food to Dayspring and the Red Cross Pantry. Holy Spirit provides personal kits for rape victims and collects clothing for the poor. Thanksgiving baskets are distributed. Its "Let Our Spirit Soar" campaign paid off the mortgage in December 1998. In 2005, the parish had more than 2,400 households.

◆ Holy Spirit Church

ST. JOHN VIANNEY
◆ FISHERS

BISHOP WILLIAM HIGI announced formation of this parish on June 26, 2005, in Fall Creek Township, Hamilton County, and appointed Father Brian Dudzinski its founding pastor. Having purchased a priest's residence in Fishers, Father Dudzinski opened a parish Web site to announce Mass times and locations and to offer parish information for St. John Vianney's community progress.

The parish used converted office space on 136th Street for its first Christmas Mass in 2005. The space also provides parish offices and a Blessed Sacrament Chapel.

◆ Bishop Higi installs Father Dudzinski
as pastor of St. John Vianney

◆ The fledgling parish's worship space

◆ Mass at St. John Vianney

◆ Converted office space houses the diocese's newest parish

ST. MARY ◆ DUNNINGTON

BISHOP JOHN BENNETT dedicated St. Mary Church on May 11, 1952. The parish's third church was erected during the pastorate of Father Francis Scheck (1949-1981). In 1892 Father Francis Lambert (1888-1918) purchased the second church's site for Nativity of the Blessed Virgin Mary, completed on July 1, 1893. This 125 x 52-foot church cost $9,000. He also built a convent across the street, remodeled the rectory and added a school in 1912.

Back in 1871, the scattered German, French, and Irish settlers in Parish Grove township and surrounding areas in Benton County found it a hardship to attend church at Kentland or Dehner's Corner. Father John Dinnen from Oxford in 1874 organized St. Michael's congregation, but because no clear title could be obtained for the site to build a church in Talbot, the site was refused. Benedictine Father Meinrad McCarthy chose a site in the middle of the Catholic settlement and constructed a 30 x 40-foot frame St. Columbkille Church for $850. After the first Mass there on Christmas Day 1876, Father Meinrad McCarthy visited St. Columbkille's from Oxford twice a month until fall of 1877.

◆ *The school in winter*

Father Francis Lang, at Oxford from 1877 to 1882, not only raised funds for a church addition, but at its completion renamed the church Holy Trinity and changed its address to Langton. The area was in the Weaver City vicinity, renamed Ambia in 1873; finally it came into Dunnington when a post office opened in 1888. In 1882, Bishop Joseph Dwenger sent Father John Grogan as Holy Trinity's first resident pastor. He erected an eight-room frame residence for $900. Father Lambert had the second church built in 1893. Since 2000, Father Donald Gross from Fowler has been administrator of St. Mary, Dunnington, where its 80 households worship.

◆ *St. Mary Church*

ST. JOHN THE BAPTIST
◆ EARL PARK

BISHOP WILLIAM HIGI dedicated Earl Park's third St. John the Baptist Church on June 8, 1997, for 74 households of 146 people. The 230-capacity, 4,700-square-foot church serving 74 households replaced the second Romanesque church damaged beyond repair in a 1993 fire. Bishop Herman Alerding had dedicated that church on September 6, 1903. The first 1880 wooden church was remodeled into a school opened in 1904 under the direction of Adrian Dominican Sisters until 1920 when Lafayette Franciscan Sisters came. After it burned down in 1925, a brick school was built and dedicated by Bishop John Noll in 1926.

Area Catholics had attended Mass at St. Anthony, Kentland, or Fowler. Father Anthony Messman organized a St. Anthony's Parish at Dehner's Corner in 1869. Its wooden church stood until 1921. In 1880, A.D. Raub and Adams Earl donated two lots for Earl Park's 300-seating capacity church, the first of any church in Earl Park. Priests from Kentland, Oxford and Fowler served the mission. A former Notre Dame chemistry professor, Holy Cross Father Thomas Vagnier, arrived in August 1888 as the parish's first resident pastor.

When Bishop Joseph Rademacher sent Father Peter Weber to Earl Park (1895-1919), adjacent lots were purchased for a new brick rectory and church. The 18,000-square-foot structure with its capacity to seat 650 made it Benton County's largest church. By the time its debt was

◆ *The second church*

met in 1920, building repairs surfaced, incurring new debts for Msgr. Aloysius Copenolle (1923-1961). During this time, about 800 people attended the new school cornerstone laying in 1925. A new seven-room convent was also built. In 1977, the parish listed 149 households. Since 1996, Kentland's pastor, Father Rob Bernotas, has administered it.

◆ *St. John the Baptist Church*

SACRED HEART OF JESUS
◆ FOWLER

BISHOP JOSEPH RADEMACHER dedicated Sacred Heart of Jesus Church on Ascension Thursday 1896. It was built after Fowler's first resident pastor, Father Antonius Henneberger, was appointed on June 29, 1889. At his arrival the parish consisted of 28 Irish, 20 Canadian and 12 German families. The first school was built in 1891. After Father Henry Hellhake's interlude (1898-1900), Father Henneberger returned and served until 1907. The parish had 131 households numbering 670 people.

In 1875, Bishop Joseph Dwenger had dedicated a frame St. John the Evangelist Church at Fowler. Priests from Oxford attended the mission from 1872, especially after Father John Dempsey (1878-1882) built a rectory there from his own means.

Sacred Heart grew rapidly as families of French-Canadian descent arrived from the St. Anne and Beaverville, Illinois, area. Father Charles Dhe served from 1907 to 1939. He built Sacred Heart Academy in 1910, which served as a boarding school and convent. Lafayette Franciscan Sisters taught in the school until 1998. Destroyed by fire in 1914, the rectory was replaced in 1915. Father Leo Dufrane added 40 feet to the church's east end by 1940. In 1946, Father Otto Peters arranged the parish Golden Jubilee celebration.

◆ *Sacred Heart of Jesus Church*

◆ *A wedding around 1997*

Father Sylvester Klein, 1949-78, completed the erection of a new convent in 1951, supervised construction of the present school in 1958 and redecorated church in 1970. Father Donald Vernon (1978-2000) continued building improvements and organized centennials for the school in 1991, and the church in 1996. In 1994, the church was again redecorated and the Rite of Christian Initiation for Adults was organized. From 1992, Sacred Heart pastors have administered St. Mary, Dunnington, as Father Donald Gross continues to do since July 2000. The parish currently has 423 households and 147 children in Sacred Heart School.

SS. PETER AND PAUL
◆ GOODLAND

BISHOP HERMAN ALERDING dedicated the present SS. Peter and Paul Church on July 12, 1903. Caring simultaneously for St. Anthony's at Dehner's Corner, in 1902 Father Gregory Zern received an assistant priest, Father Francis King, who resided at Goodland. From the eight pioneer families served by Father Joseph Stephan from Rensselaer in 1863, the congregation grew to 15 households by 1880. Congregation trustees Peter Traudeau, Peter Brook and Paul Weishaar persuaded missionary Father John Hoss to build a frame church in Goodland. As the parish grew to 50 households in 1900, Father Zern determined the mission had matured for Father King's arrival. Until then priests from St. Anthony's or Kentland cared for the Goodland and Morroco missions. Father Joseph Bilstein (1899-1900) had built Sacred Heart of Jesus Church at Morocco.

Bishop Alerding appointed Father Zern first resident pastor of SS. Peter and Paul Church on October 1, 1903. The church seats 350. Father Ignatius Zircher (1905-1912) built the rectory in 1908. In 1911, the parish Mount Calvary Cemetery was established from Mathew Moran's gift. Father Ambrose Kohne came to SS. Peter and Paul's in 1933, serving until his retirement in 1963 to Kokomo Good Samaritan Home. Father Carl Eckert was sent as parish administrator prior to serving as pastor from 1964 to 1968. SS. Peter and Paul's first parish pastoral council was installed in 1969.

When SS. Peter and Paul's grew to 176 households in 1976, Father Thomas Timmerman (1973-1978)

◆ *SS. Peter and Paul Church*

described the Newton County parish as a combination of the Gothic church building and its people putting their time and energy into SS. Peter and Paul's ministries and receiving the sacraments to help them on their pilgrim journey. Currently Kentland's pastor, Father Rob Bernotas, administers SS. Peter and Paul Parish of 69 households.

◆ *The sanctuary before renovation*

◆ *Victory Noll catechist teaching, 1963*

ST. JOSEPH ◆ KENTLAND

◆ *St. Joseph School*

◆ *The sanctuary in 1988*

BISHOP JOHN LUERS appointed Father Anthony Messman Kentland's first resident pastor in 1870. In 1872, a rectory and a school were built. The school, taught by lay teachers, closed, and then reopened in 1885. In 1887, Lafayette Franciscan Sisters followed by Sisters of St. Joseph of Tipton ran the school for which a new building was erected in 1927. After closing in 1970, the school reopened in 1980. The Sisters of St. Joseph of the Third Order of St. Francis took over until their departure and its closing in 2001.

About 15 Catholic families in a 12-mile radius formed Kentland's first church visited monthly by Father George Hamilton from Logansport (1861-1864) and Father Joseph Stephan from Rensselaer (1864-1870). Father Hamilton used the courthouse or Kent's Hotel for Mass until Father Stephan built the first frame church in 1864.

From Kentland, Father Messman (1870-1880) cared for Remington, Earl Park, St. Anthony's and Goodland. Father William Miller (1883-1891) built the second and present brick St. Joseph Church in

1888. With a seating capacity of 300, the church contains the main altar of the mission church. From 1902 to 1903, Precious Blood Missionaries were St. Joseph's pastors. Father Charles Stetter served in St. Joseph Parish from 1903 to 1929. He built a rectory, a school, and a convent, and repaired and redecorated the church. Daily he taught church history at the school. His hour-long homilies on the Bible merited Father Joachim Baker's eulogy to declare, "He was a man of Scripture." Another priest who served an extensive term at St. Joseph's was Father Edward Fallon (1939-1964). Both Fathers Stetter's and Fallon's bodies are buried in St. Joseph Cemetery.

Today St. Joseph's 210 households consist of 502 persons. Kentland's pastor Father Rob Bernotas cares for parishes at Earl Park and Goodland.

◆ *St. Joseph Church*

◆ *St. Augusta Church*

ST. AUGUSTA ◆ LAKE VILLAGE

ISHOP RAYMOND GALLAGHER dedicated the renovated St. Augusta Church on October 23, 1977. In 1947, Ray and Clare Churchill had presented land for a church. During Father Charles Scholl's pastorate (1957-1970), a church was built and 14 people were baptized on May 31, 1958. At Father Scholl's retirement at 83, the parish boasted 50 households. In 1970, Father William Higi from Lafayette became administrator. In 1974, St. Augusta's facilities doubled the building's original size. By 1977, the parish had 147 households.

Originally, in 1910 the Adolph Yott family had engaged Goodland's priest for occasional home Masses at Lake Village. In 1911-15, Lowell's pastor came. In 1915, a former school was purchased and remodeled into St. Agnes Church, used till 1940. A 1916 First Communion photo shows 13 children from 4 families with Lowell's priest. In the 1940s, Father John Woods resumed occasional Masses until 1957, referring to Lake Village as the "Mission of St. Theresa Church in Shelby."

When Msgr. Higi was to be installed as fifth Bishop of the Diocese of Lafayette-in-Indiana, Father Donald Gross was appointed second resident pastor. He purchased rectory property and additional church acreage. While Fathers Michael McKinley (1993-1997) and Ambrose Ziegler (1997-2000) served there, interior church renovations were made. The Ladies Guild purchased a lighted announcement sign to post outside. Additional renovations continued during Father John Cummings' pastorate (2000-2004), which included a sanctuary upgrade and new custom furnishings created by Kadar and Son Wood Shop through fundraising by the Ladies' Guild. Bishop Higi dedicated the new altar on June 22, 2001.

With Benedictine Father Stephen Snoich its present pastor, St. Augusta is currently comprised of 255 households or 740 persons.

◆ *Father Scholl at the baptismal font, 1966*

ST. CHARLES BORROMEO
◆ OTTERBEIN

BISHOP HERMAN ALERDING dedicated St. Charles Borromeo Church on June 8, 1902. The Gothic brick edifice seated 200 and served 61 households. Membership grew to 90 by 1952 and 144 by 2005.

The parish originated in connection with the Ditch Church in Pine Township. From 1860 to 1863, Father Joseph Stephan had celebrated Mass at various Benton County sites. When a church was built in Oxford, people attended there. In 1873, a church and hall were erected near the State Ditch. In 1876, a windstorm destroyed the church, but the hall was used until Fowler's priest completed St. Bridget's second frame church in 1879. Priests from Lafayette and Oxford ministered irregularly to the mainly Irish railroad workers. With a population increase in 1896, Oxford's priest built a stately brick church to seat 325 for 43 households or 245 persons. On July 10, 1901, Bishop Alerding

◈ *St. Charles Borromeo Church*

appointed Father Charles McCabe St. Bridget's first resident pastor with an Otterhein mission. In this year St. Bridget's location was named Barrydale.

In 1901, Bishop Alerding assigned Father McCabe who laid the cornerstone for a church in October. In 1931, Bishop John Noll commissioned Father Joseph Keating to reside at Otterbein with Barrydale as its mission. Father Keating prepared a building fund for a new rectory, which Father Ladislaus Krause (1937-1943) completed by 1939. He also satisfied the church building debt. Father Emil Schweier (1943-1948) arranged for the Lafayette Franciscan Sisters to conduct religious education from first grade to high school.

St. Charles Borromeo's priest was pastor of Otterbein and Barrydale until 1991 when a lightning storm struck and set St. Bridget Church afire beyond restoration. Since then its parishioners have been part of St. Charles Borromeo Parish. In 2005, the parish was clustered with St. Patrick, Oxford.

◈ *Bishop Gallagher at parish's 75th anniversary celebration, 1977*

ST. PATRICK ◆ OXFORD

◆ *St. Patrick Church*

◆ *The church interior, 1953*

St. Mary's, Lafayette (1894-1927), to preside at the rededication on August 26, 1904. The parish had about 30 households. During Father James Fitzgerald's pastorate, 1927-32, St. Patrick was again redecorated and a second Sunday Mass was added to accommodate its 55 households. By 1944, the parish had grown to 98 households or 398 persons.

In 1998, the church renovation begun by Father Theodore Rothrock (1991-1998) was completed. The church interior received Father Donald Eder's hand-hewn wooden furnishings. With Father Eder's design, parishioner Gary Deno constructed other furnishings, including the altar. St. Patrick's people not only funded, but also participated in the 2001 redecoration. Father Eder and John Brost's leadership promote an annual trip to assist the needy in Mexico. In 2005, St. Patrick Church, seating 196, serves 169 households or 479 persons.

BISHOP JOHN LUERS sent Father C. J. O'Callaghan to be Oxford's first resident pastor (1867-1870). The Oxford mission at Benton County's seat till 1873 was served from Lafayette (1863-1867) when Father Edmund Kilroy laid a church foundation and cornerstone. Until the railroad reached Oxford, materials were hauled 25 miles from Lafayette. Irish railroad workers settled there as northern Benton County became colonized with German, French and Canadian immigrants.

From 1860 to 1863, Father Joseph Stephan of St. Boniface, Lafayette, had celebrated Mass at a vacant Disciples of Christ church, the county courthouse or a school. From Lafayette's St. Mary's, Bishop Luers sent Father John Dinnen (1870-1876) whom he had ordained a year before at St. Patrick Church, Chicago, to build a rectory and complete the building of St. Patrick Church, Oxford, begun by Fathers O'Callaghan and Stephan as the county's first Catholic church.

When St. Patrick's was extensively renovated and decorated, Father William Miller invited Father Dinnen, pastor of

◆ *The complex from the air, 1989*

SORROWFUL MOTHER
◆ WHEATFIELD

◆ *First Communion class in 1943*

BISHOP JOHN CARBERRY dedicated the present Sorrowful Mother Church on October 14, 1962. When Bishop John Bennett sent Father Sylvester Klein as Wheatfield's first resident pastor in 1945, the second Sorrowful Mother mission church was in use. Precious Blood Father Dominic Shunk from the Indian Normal School, Rensselaer, organized a group of six households to build a 12 x16 log church. It was dedicated in 1887. In 1889, another frame church seating 150 was erected for 12 households. By 1907, 25 households or 87 persons received bi-monthly ministry from Precious Blood Missionaries of Saint Joseph's College, Rensselaer.

Father Joseph Stephan from San Pierre, Starke County, celebrated Masses at William Grube Sr.'s home, 1872-1884; the Eagle Hotel hall, 1884-1886; and the Heil Log Cabin School, 1886-1887. While early settlers were primarily Pennsylvania Dutch, other Germans arrived to settle the Indian Ridge. After the World Wars, a variety of ethnic groups from Lake, LaPorte and Porter counties spilled into Jasper County.

◆ *Centennial Quilt made by women of the parish*

From 1911-1921, Sorrowful Mother was a mission of St. Edward's, Lowell, then from 1921-1944, of St. Mary's, Kouts. In 1937, Father Augustyn Kondziela of Kouts celebrated the mission's Golden Jubilee. At Father Klein's arrival, Don Bosco Youth Center serving the entire community was built in 1945. When a fire in 1960 burned it down, the parishioners began to envision a new church and hall.

While Father Donald Hardebeck was Sorrowful Mother's pastor (1949-1957), the parish started

St. Cecilia mission at DeMotte. On July 11, 1982, ground was broken for an addition to the parish hall. Bishop Raymond Gallagher dedicated the unit as Klein Hall on October 31, 1982.

With 350 seats, Sorrowful Mother serves 256 households or 997 persons. The year 2005 marked the 33rd year of its annual fish fry.

◆ *Sorrowful Mother Church*

ST. FRANCIS XAVIER
◆ ATTICA

Bishop Joseph Rademacher of Nashville dedicated St. Francis Xavier Church on June 21, 1891. The present 104 x 40-foot church of handmade bricks replaced Attica's first frame church, which Father Joseph Stephan built in 1862, a year before Father Rademacher was sent as its first resident pastor in 1863. From 1849 to 1860, priests from Lafayette and Crawfordsville offered occasional Masses at private homes or local halls for the Catholic Wabash railroad- and bridge-laborers.

After the church's dedication, Father Charles Lemper turned the 1870s school addition into a Sisters' residence and made the old church into a two-room school that lasted a year. Father Lemper also had built the Victorian rectory, which Father Edward Matuszak remodeled in 1983 after the 1979 church renovation.

On April 29, 1954, Bishop John Bennett blessed a new parish hall. On September 15 during the 1954 Marian Year, Father Richard Puetz dedicated an outdoor Blessed Mother shrine. The church interior was renovated in 1962 with an electronic bell system and carillon tower. The carillon was replaced during the 1990 church renovation when shrines to St. Francis Xavier and the Crucified Lord were added to the parish grounds. Father Charles Kline (1995-2005) oversaw many improvements to the facilities, while he was also missioned as pastor of St. Joseph, Covington in 2000.

◆ *St. Francis Xavier Church*

St. Francis Xavier Ladies Guild, originally the Altar and Rosary Society, does much to carry out God's work. In addition to its weekly sewing circle for overseas missions and the "Pope's Warehouse," its members serve at socials and funerals, contact shut-ins, provide for the needy in Fountain and Warren counties and hold fundraisers for worthy causes. The parish's 192 households consist of 467 people.

◆ *Interior of the church, 1962*

◆ *100ᵗʰ anniversary of church dedication, 1991*

ST. JOSEPH ◆ COVINGTON

BISHOP JOHN LUERS dedicated St. Joseph Church in October 1867. In 1860, Father Joseph Stephan had laid its brick foundation for 40 households of Wabash canal and railroad workers. Although Crawfordsville's Father Edward O'Flaherty visited the mission in 1859, his absence brought priests from Attica to care for Covington and its missions at Coal Creek-Shoddy's Mills (1864-1888), Veedersburg (1897-1946) and Stringtown.

Covington's resident pastor Father Henry Plaster built the rectory in 1880. In 1945, it was replaced with a National Home trucked from Lafayette and laid on a full basement by parishioners who were supervised by Stanley Gott. On October 8, 1949, Dr. T.T. Suzuki delivered a newborn parishioner Louis Frazer in this rectory. Although he was a native Japanese-American, Dr. Suzuki was not allowed to practice in local hospitals because of post-World War II prejudice.

Vernon Hall, built in 1969 for religious education classes and meetings, was gutted by a lightning fire in 1979 and completely rebuilt. Although a nearby house was purchased for a possible school in 1979, like the wood frame church

◆ *St. Joseph in earlier days*

addition built for a school in 1875, a fire destroyed it. Its site became the church's east parking lot.

When Father Donald Tracey was named resident pastor (1987-1988), Richard Warner made and installed bookracks on the back of the church pews. From 1946, St. Joseph Parish has been administered from Attica or Lafayette, although Father Leroy Kinnaman (1995-2000) also served as its pastor while he was the Wabash College Newman chaplain at Crawfordsville. Father Kinnaman had a new parish hall constructed and Vernon Education Center was divided into classrooms. Since 2000, the parish is cared for by the priest from St. Francis Xavier, Attica. Its 60 households consist of 110 people.

◆ *St. Joseph Church*

◆ *St. Bernard Church*

ST. BERNARD ◆ CRAWFORDSVILLE

◆ *The Newman Center at Wabash College*

Bishop William Higi dedicated the fourth St. Bernard Church on June 29, 1986. With a seating capacity of 450 and built during Father David Clifford's pastorate (1978-1990), it meets all post-Vatican II liturgical guidelines. It replaced the third church with a seating capacity of 350 and the school, which Msgr. Henry Ward built and Bishop John Carberry dedicated on June 29, 1958, when the parish relocated from Pike and Washington streets to its present 16-acre campus in the 1300 block of East Main Street.

Father Edward Walters (1868-1878) built the second Gothic church seating 400, which Bishop Joseph Dwenger dedicated on September 17, 1876. The Holy Cross Sisters operated St. Charles Academy on Main and Grant streets for girls. The boys attended school in the church sacristy.

While Scottish and German settlers coming to Montgomery County were initially served by priests from Lafayette, in 1859 Bishop John Luers appointed Father Edward O'Flaherty Crawfordsville's first resident pastor. He and parishioners hand-built the first log church, which sat 200. Father Charles Maugin modernized the building, replacing its twin fireplaces with an iron stove and installing windows. Father John Dinnen (1878-1894) built the brick rectory. The log church was recycled into a sexton's house at Calvary Cemetery acquired from the Elston family in 1872.

St. Bernard's Wabash College Newman Center ministry began when Father Kenneth Raczek initiated its Newman Apostolate (1960-1963). Its sister parish is St. Francis Xavier in Carrefour Sanon, Haiti. During Father Paul Graf's service (1990-1994), a Ministry of Care for the sick and shut-ins was begun and the Renew program introduced. Through a parish planning process, Father Melvin Bennett (1994-2005) re-opened St. Bernard School. In addition to its religious education program, the parish of 550 households educates pupils from kindergarten to the fifth grade.

◆ *Calvary Cemetery*

◆ *Interior view*

Cathedral interior from the choir

CATHEDRAL OF ST. MARY OF THE IMMACULATE CONCEPTION ◆ LAFAYETTE

BISHOP WILLIAM HIGI dedicated the renovated Gothic Cathedral of St. Mary of the Immaculate Conception on April 26, 2001. Since 1866, St. Mary had been a parish church developed from Lafayette's SS. Mary and Martha Church, which originated in 1844 and whose missionaries evangelized most of the present diocese. Since 1944, the church has been continually renovated to serve as a diocesan cathedral.

The church's latest renovation took place after its sesquicentennial in 1993. Father Richard Weisenberger and the parish planning committee remodeled the former convent into parish offices in 1996. Because in 1998 Bishop Higi decided to keep this church as the diocesan cathedral, by 2001 it was renovated inside and out. A social hall was built where the St. Ignatius Academy building (1861-1936) stood before it became a parking lot when the parochial school was built. Msgr. Michael Chapman oversaw the building of the school, which Bishop John

Noll dedicated on September 7, 1936. From 1867 to 1895, Holy Cross Brothers taught the boys and from 1858 to 1895, the Sisters of Providence, the girls, and then all the children of the parish. Fashioned in 1877, the church's stained-glass windows are the only items unaffected by St. Mary's many renovations. Its steeple was finished in 1898.

Although SS. Mary and Martha started with 15 to 25 households, even after St. Boniface was formed from it in 1853, by 1859 it had 2,500 parishioners when Father Edmund Kilroy began St. Mary's construction. With the gift of the William Burnett Davis estate, Father George Hamilton completed it for dedication on August 15, 1866. Father John Dinnen had its bell tower and steeple finished in 1898. Father Dinnen insisted on having boundaries for St. Mary's and St. Ann's. In 1894, after he received Bishop Joseph Rademacher's boundaries, strictly to be observed with no exceptions, by 1902 so

◈ The church interior after its 1976 renovation

◈ Funeral of Father E.P. Walters, 1894

◈ Exterior view of the Cathedral

many exceptions had been made that his petition to the bishop resulted in St. Ann's expanded boundaries and his appeal to the apostolic delegation in Washington, D.C. There is no record of a response.

During the 1930s, Father Lawrence Monahan had the church's exterior brick covered with imitation stone. Msgr. Chapman saw to the sanctuary's expansion in 1944 for the installation of the Diocese's first Bishop John Bennett on January 10, 1945. Charles Ball donated the Bishop's chair, faldstool, and vestments, among other items. In 1957, Bishop John Carberry had the statue of Our Lady installed in front of the church. For the renovation of 1977, Msgr. Fred Potthoff introduced a Byzantine tile mosaic of the Tree of Life over the tabernacle and replaced the crucified Christ on the sanctuary cross with a risen Christ.

Until 1878, St. Mary's assistant priests were missionary pastors of numerous missions. Father Patrick Crosson

(1878-1880) was it first parish assistant or associate pastor. After St. Ann was formed in 1884 and St. Lawrence in 1895, in 1907 the parish had 255 households of 965 people. Since West Lafayette's St. Thomas Aquinas' opening in 1951 and Blessed Sacrament's in 1957, St. Mary has continued to grow, comprising today 1,227 households of 3,160 people.

St. Mary's parishioners have shown leadership in many local and national Catholic organizations and good works. Its parishioners share in supportive aspects of ministries to Lafayette Catholic Schools, St. Elizabeth Medical Center, Precious Blood Monastery, St. Vincent de Paul Conference and the Newman Apostolate at St. Thomas Aquinas. The parish maintains complete religious education, music, liturgy, and Order of Christian Initiation for Adults programs. The parish's present full administrative staff reflects a heritage of parishioners participating in many societies and organizations.

ST. BONIFACE ◆ LAFAYETTE

◆ St. Boniface Church

◆ Interior view, 1997

Increased enrollment in 1999 required kindergarten through third grade's continuing at St. Mary and fourth through sixth at St. Boniface. Seventh and eighth formed a junior high at Central Catholic High School.

Diocesan priests served St. Boniface until 1866 when Bishop Luers placed the Franciscan Friars of the Cincinnati Province in charge. They served the parish until withdrawing in 1991. In 1986, Bishop William Higi designated the parish for the Lafayette Hispanic community. Since 1994, Father Timothy Alkire has continued working with the many active societies. The parish has 1,010 households of 3,116 persons.

BISHOP MAURICE DE ST. PALAIS sent Father William Doyle on December 25, 1853, to meet with German Americans in SS. Mary and Martha Church to establish Lafayette's second parish. By 1854, the 77 charter parishioners worshiped in a brick St. Boniface Church on North 10th Street until the Ninth and North Street location could be procured. The site's graves were moved to Gerald Ostendorf's land donation for St. Joseph Cemetery. On December 10, 1865, Bishop John Luers dedicated the second and present St. Boniface Church. On September 24, 1899, the apostolic delegate, Archbishop Sebastiano Martinelli, consecrated this church the year after Bishop Joseph Rademacher blessed the new 21-acre St. Boniface Cemetery on September 17.

The old church received a second story and served as a school until 1908. Ursulines from Louisville, Kentucky, taught at St. Bonifacius Academy until 1877. They were followed by the Franciscan Sisters. In 1909, a new St. Boniface parochial school was dedicated by former pupil, Franciscan Provincial Father Rudolph Bonner. In 1975, St. Boniface and St. Mary Schools consolidated. Kindergarten through fifth grade attended St. Mary and sixth through eighth, St. Boniface.

◆ Stations of the Cross

◆ 1965 Homecoming Banquet

◆ *St. Lawrence Church*

ST. LAWRENCE ◆ LAFAYETTE

BISHOP HERMAN ALERDING dedicated St. Lawrence Church on June 17, 1923. The Romanesque brick and stone church that seated 475 succeeded the 350-seating capacity church and school edifice that Bishop Joseph Rademacher dedicated on November 8, 1896. More than 100 households, mainly from St. Boniface, and about 20 from St. Mary's were its early parishioners attracted to employment at the Monon Railroad shop yards that moved from New Albany to Lafayette's Linwood annex in 1895.

The Franciscan Friars were given charge of founding the parish of St. Lawrence, deacon and martyr. Its free parochial school, supported by a school society to which every parishioner belonged, opened in September 1896 with three Franciscan Sisters teaching its eight grades. St. Lawrence High School filled the 1896 structure from 1923 to 1928 until St. Francis High School for Girls opened behind St. Elizabeth Hospital. The parochial school and its athletic programs have flourished through the years. The Franciscan Friars and Sisters served the parish until 1991 and 1992, respectively. From 1991 to 1995, Father Leroy Kinnaman served as its first diocesan priest.

On March 23, 1996, the church interior was damaged by a Saturday evening fire. That Saturday, Mass was held in the gym while about 100 firemen extinguished the fire. It was a coincidence that the parish's centennial occurred with St. Lawrence in its original building

St. Lawrence Parish and School continue to grow. With 1,134 households of 3,178 persons, St. Lawrence created more space for students with an addition to its school and a new pre-school in 2002. In 2005, the parish built a new social hall with an additional 8,000 square feet for future growth. Faithful to its past, St. Lawrence Parish lives with a vision for its future.

◆ *First Communion class and "angels," 1916*

99

◆ *Church of the Blessed Sacrament*

CHURCH OF THE BLESSED SACRAMENT
◆ WEST LAFAYETTE

BISHOP JOHN CARBERRY dedicated the Church of the Blessed Sacrament on April 1, 1962. On September 3, 1957, Bishop John Bennett erected the parish with Father Donald Hardebeck as its founding pastor. On July 21, its first Mass was held at St. Thomas Aquinas, and three days later, it held its organizational meeting. For four years, the 290 founding families worshipped at St. Thomas, Morton School gymnasium, and the State Street Jacques Building.

Since Bishop Carberry had given permission to move the church from its Salisbury and Robinson streets site to Navajo Street in the Wabash Shores subdivision, its church groundbreaking was held there on March 6, 1961, and the cornerstone laid on June 16. An east wing was added in 1976.

After Father David Douglas arrived in 1985, an outdoor Shrine of Our Lady of Lourdes was constructed in 1992. On Aug. 14, 1995, Bishop William Higi dedicated an addition, doubling the church's original size. It contains chapels, a reconciliation room, a new entrance and gathering space, a more adequate library, a large dining hall and kitchen, meeting rooms, a nursery, offices, and an elevator. The Parish Center basement was reconfigured for religious education classrooms, youth ministry, adult education and retreats.

Blessed Sacrament lives its mission in many ways, including ecumenical hosting of Jubilee Christmas, assistance to the community's poor and support for St. Margaret Mary sister parish in Bogota, Colombia. The current physical structure offers facilities for a growing parish of 746 households, more than double its 1957 households who prayed on rubber kneeling pads in a school gymnasium. Blessed Sacrament's first parish event, the "Jonah Fish Fry," continues to bring the parish together each August almost 50 years later.

◆ *A parish family day*

◆ *St. Thomas Aquinas Church*

ST. THOMAS AQUINAS
◆ WEST LAFAYETTE

BISHOP JOHN BENNETT dedicated St. Thomas Aquinas Center as a Catholic student chapel at Purdue University on April 9, 1951. Students no longer had to trek across the Wabash River to St. Mary Cathedral from which evolved a 1906 Catholic Club, a 1917 Phi Kappa Fraternity and a 1927 Newman Club. St. Mary's assistant, Father Leo Pursley, had the Newman Club chartered at the university. Thus when World War II G.I. Bill enrollment surged, Bishop Bennett made Father Thomas Heilman the students' vicar. Our Sunday Visitor Foundation's grant and a Cathedral appeal enabled Bishop Bennett to purchase the State Street property.

With the 1957 advent of Father Leo Piguet and his associate, Father Leo Haigerty, a Notre Dame University credit course was developed. St. Thomas Aquinas became the preferred name in 1962. Communion Breakfasts, group meetings, lectures and social gatherings met in Newman Hall. In 1963, adjacent property was purchased. Bishop John Carberry dedicated the expanded St. Thomas Aquinas Church on May 3, 1964. The design that provided a seating capacity of 1,100 received the first-place award for church renovation from the North American Liturgical Conference in 1964. Area residents' participation, especially the Cathedral Christian Family Movement's parties in the 1960s, enriched the already diverse parish. Two or three priests met the needs of its several thousand members.

St. Thomas parishioners participate in Lafayette Urban Ministry, Jubilee Christmas, tutoring, overnight hosting of the homeless and marching in the Hunger Hike. Since 1990, several groups have traveled to a sister parish in Baudin, Haiti.

Since 2000, Dominican Friars of the Order of Preachers with a full supporting staff serve the vibrant parish of 821 households and 5,558 students. St. Thomas is that home away from home so valuable to Purdue University students.

◆ *Church attendance in earlier years*

BISHOP'S RESIDENCE

CATHOLIC PASTORAL CENTER

CHANCERY BUILDING

PAPAL BULL CREATING
THE DIOCESE

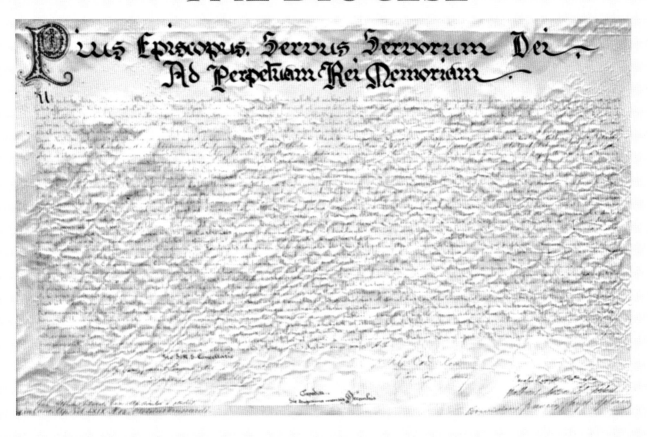

Pius Episcopus, Servus Servorum Dei.
Ad Perpetuam Rei Memoriam.

ST. JOSEPH ◆ DELPHI

ISHOP MAURICE DE ST. PALAIS dedicated the early American Gothic St. Joseph Church on February 9, 1861, in the presence of Bishop John Luers. Priests had visited the Wabash River town from its start, especially from Lafayette and Logansport in 1854 until Father George Hamilton completed the church that Father John Vahey started in spring 1860. Its 150 parishioners of Irish, German and French descent worshipped in an old brick schoolhouse dating back to 1857 on Indiana Street until the church was dedicated.

Bishop Luers appointed Father August Oechtering Delphi's first resident pastor on May 26, 1861. Father John Bleckmann's arrival in 1885 saw the installation of an organ and bell donated by John Ruffing and Henry Swigman. The bell was christened in honor of Bishop Luers and the donors' baptismal names: The John Henry. Sisters of Providence operated St. Joseph School from 1876 to 1901 and Sisters of St. Joseph of Tipton from 1901 to 1970. Mrs. Irma Crosby, who taught there for 15 years, merited the distinction of being the only lay teacher in the school's history.

The church steeple was completed in 1899 after being redecorated in 1894. Other church remodeling occurred in 1941, 1954, 1963, 1971, 1983 and 1991. The renovation under Father Donald Hardebeck in 1991 not only installed new furnishings, but added a Blessed Sacrament chapel and prayer garden along the Monroe

◆ St. Joseph Church

Street side of the church. Honan Hall, a gift from Mr. and Mrs. Burton Honan in 1967, was dedicated by Bishop Raymond Gallagher on February 25, 1968. St. Joseph religious education program includes grades K through 12. With a full staff and both liturgical and social ministries including prayer and Eucharistic Adoration, the more than 700 parishioners today grow together as a Christian community through liturgy, prayer, and action.

◆ St. Joseph Church, dedicated 1861

◆ The last day at St. Joseph School, 1970

◈ *St. Francis Solano Church*

ST. FRANCIS SOLANO - ST. HENRY

◆ FRANCESVILLE - MEDARYVILLE

BISHOP WILLIAM HIGI established the parish of St. Francis Solano-St. Henry, Francesville-Medaryville, on January 13, 1991. Both churches share a common history as Monon railroad mission stops for priests from Lafayette, Winamac, and Reynolds from 1855 to 1878. Frame churches were built for a dozen households at Francesville, 1867, and Medaryville, 1868.

In 1991, St. Francis Solano-St. Henry Parish had 68 households (34 households each). In 2005, the parish had 61 households.

Between 1878 and 1888, Franciscan Friars from Reynolds rode the Monon to these missions, calling Medaryville St. Mary's. Then Fort Wayne diocesan priests

◈ *125th anniversary, 1993*

◈ *1867 Francesville Catholic mission church*

105

ST. JOAN OF ARC ◆ KOKOMO

◆ *St. Joan of Arc mission chapel and school, built 1922*

◆ *Interior view, 2004*

BISHOP WILLIAM HIGI blessed the third St. Joan of Arc Church relocated to South County Road 200 West on January 4, 2004. The 93,000-square-foot, three-level edifice of concrete pre-cast panels has a granite entrance canopy, green-tinted architectural glass and a structural steel framing system set on three acres of its 29.7-acre campus. Five acres constitute the cove of a 50-acre lake. Its worship area seats 628. The building was remodeled to include 12 classrooms plus auxiliary rooms. St. Joan's more than 1,500 households consist of approximately 4,106 persons active in 80 parish and community ministries.

The parish site was transferred from its South Purdum Street location where Archbishop Paul Schulte of Indianapolis had dedicated the parish's second church on May 7, 1950, after Bishop John Bennett laid its cornerstone on September 5, 1949. Father Francis Niesen (1946-1970) was assigned to Kokomo to replace the red brick St. Joan of Arc Chapel and School that

St. Patrick pastor, Father Robert Pratt, had built in 1922 to serve 140 households. St. Patrick's priests cared for St. Joan of Arc Chapel until Bishop John Noll sent Father John Dapp in 1927 as its first resident pastor. At Father Dennis O'Keeffe's assignment in 1998, the parish planning council recommended the purchase of the former Conseco Insurance Company site on December 19, 2002.

The red brick first church and school building was razed in 1986 after the parish purchased the Palmer Building in 1985. In 1994, St. Joan of Arc and St. Patrick schools merged. Its two campuses house preschool through second grade at St. Patrick Building, and third through eighth grades at the St. Joan of Arc Building. On June 21, 2005, the parish opened a new St. Vincent de Paul Conference Thrift Store, replacing its 1975 Good Samaritan Store.

◆ *St. Joan of Arc Church*

ST. PATRICK ◆ KOKOMO

◆ *Interior view*

◆ *St. Patrick Church*

B ISHOP HERMAN ALERDING dedicated the present Gothic Bedford stone St. Patrick Church on May 21, 1911. On November 28, 1918, Bishop Alerding consecrated the church after its debt was paid off in 118 months.

From 1844, priests from Lafayette, Logansport, and Peru had ministered to Catholics settling the newly organized Howard County, while Father George Hamilton built the first St. Patrick frame church in 1859 on a lot donated by Kokomo's mayor and another purchased by the Church at Washington and Broadway streets. When Father Patrick Frawley became Kokomo's first resident pastor in 1869, the parish had grown to 40 households. At Father Francis Lordemann's appointment in 1873, parish growth required replacing the mission church with Kokomo's largest church in 1877. A 56 x 115-foot, brick church that sat 700 was built. The mission church was remodeled into St. Francis Academy, demolished when St. Patrick School was erected in 1962. In 1994, St. Patrick and St. Joan of Arc schools merged.

Since by 1905, the parish had increased in size, Father Lordemann undertook construction of the present 160 x 80-foot church with a 176-foot main tower and 130-foot south tower. The church contains two windows executed by the Kokomo Opalescent Glass Works, the third largest stained glass windows in the United States. In 1922, St. Patrick began St. Joan of Arc mission in south Kokomo. It became Kokomo's second parish in 1927.

In 1975, Msgr. Arthur Sego oversaw an eight-year project renovating the church interior. Since Father Theodore Dudzinski's arrival in 2002, parishioners constructed and furnished a Blessed Sacrament Chapel for perpetual adoration. It was dedicated on June 22, 2003. On August 15, 2005, Bishop William Higi rededicated the church's 2004 interior and exterior renovation. St. Patrick Parish today has about 1,000 households of 2,599 parishioners.

◆ *Church rededication, 2005*

◆ *The Pieta*

109

ST. ANNE ◆ MONTEREY

◆ *Statue of St. Anne and the church's original bell*

◆ *St. Anne Church*

Bishop Joseph Dwenger dedicated the brick, Gothic St. Anne Church in May 1884 on lots Precious Blood Father George Fleisch had purchased in 1882 in Monterey, formerly known as Buena Vista. A frame mission church was built near four wetland acres deeded to Bishop Maurice de St. Palais for a Catholic cemetery in 1852. Priests from Plymouth and Winamac alternately cared for it till Bishop Dwenger entrusted it to the Precious Blood Missionaries from Winamac or Pulaski, Indian Creek Township.

In 1888, Bishop Dwenger sent the diocesan priest Father Charles Thiele as its first resident pastor. A brick parsonage was built in 1889 and Holy Family School served the parish from 1895 to 1969. The school reopened as St. Anne's School and ran from 1980 to 2003. In 1889, a new cemetery was purchased west of town.

Over the years St. Anne has been remodeled and expanded. In the 1930s, Father John Schall had men of the parish hand-dig the present church basement. Father Robert Sorg (1970-1973) purchased and installed a shrine of St. Anne next to the rectory. Father Dominic Young (1992-2001) donated stained-glass windows for the church front doors that Father Sorg had installed in the early 1970s. The cross from St. Anne's steeple that was erected in memory of Robert and Helen (Sutter) Sell had to be taken down in 1971 to be refinished in 1997-98 and set on the churchyard side.

In 2005, the parish had 124 households of 285 persons. Considering that the 2004 population of Monterey was 228, there are more Catholics in its parish than town residents. The parish's faith-filled history remembers its former missions at Rochester, Culver, and Kouts that have all become flourishing parishes.

◆ *St. Anne School, closed in 2003*

◆ *Interior view after renovation in the early 1960s*

◆ *Our Lady of the Lakes Church*

OUR LADY OF THE LAKES
◆ MONTICELLO

B ISHOP JOHN CARBERRY dedicated the contemporary style glass and stone, A-frame Our Lady of the Lakes Church on May 27, 1962. Today's White County seat parish of 350 households with a headcount of 900 welcomes hundreds of summer parishioners enjoying its Lakes Shafer and Freeman on the Tippecanoe River.

An 1898 History of White County relates that a frame St. Mary Catholic Church graced Monticello in 1895. The Franciscan Friars from Reynolds built it in 1879. The priest from Kentland had been attending Monticello since 1871. Prior to that, priests from Logansport (1864-1870) and Father Joseph Stephan from St. Boniface, Lafayette, in 1859 gathered Catholics for worship. The 1883 Catholic Directory describes St. Mary's as having 60 German- and English-speaking persons. It had 75 by 1889 when the Franciscans left Reynolds, and it too became a mission of Remington. After 1905, Monticello Catholics traveled to Reynolds until May 14, 1945, when Father Francis Libert began using Monticello Odd Fellows Hall for Sunday Mass. By May 1946, 35 households pledged to build a church. On August 29, 1948, Bishop John Bennett dedicated Our Lady of the Lakes basement church, making it a mission of Reynolds.

Father Robert Fosselman was named the first resident pastor in 1952, although the modern style rectory was not finished until 1954. As the parish grew, Father Fosselman planned a larger church. Its construction began in 1961 during Father Richard Puetz's pastorate. It was dedicated in 1962. When Father Fosselman again served the parish between 1971 and 1982, the former basement church was made the foundation for a meeting-banquet hall and the lower level was renovated into religious education classrooms.

Our Lady of the Lakes parishioners admire their forebears in the faith whose selfless cooperation with the Holy Spirit has provided a heritage of solid foundation.

◆ *The "basement church" dedicated in 1947*

113

ST. CHARLES BORROMEO
◆ PERU

Bishop John Luers dedicated St. Charles Borromeo Church on December 8, 1867. Parishioners had built the Gothic style church from stone culled to form bricks from the Mississinewa River near Peoria, Miami County. They harvested timber after they used farm soil to fill in the corner lot on Fifth Street. This building replaced the frame church Bishop Simon Bruté allowed to be built in 1838 at the site Father Stephen Badin had purchased in 1831. Priests from Logansport served the mission monthly. In 1859, Father George Hamilton bought St. Charles' Cemetery acreage. Bishop Luers appointed Father Bernard Force Peru's first resident pastor on April 15, 1860.

St. Charles frame church was renovated for school use. A 1922 fund drive raised the present school, which Bishop John Noll dedicated in April 1931. Many church and school improvements followed, including the addition of frescoes and Bavarian stained-glass windows, a 187-foot spire, an organ and side altars. In 1907, the parish had 250 households of 1,100 people.

Another major church renovation was done in 1973 when Bishop Raymond Gallagher rededicated the church on August 26. The exterior has also seen renovation, including stucco covering its original red brick. Eventually the parish purchased all but one property in the block with the church on the southeast corner and the school on the southwest.

St. Charles' 565 households of 1,201 people today continue its long history of community service. In 1963 it began its migrant worker ministry. Other outreach includes a prison ministry to Miami Correctional Facility, Bunker Hill, Birthright, St. Vincent de Paul Society Thrift Store, and Miami County Helping Hands. The parish continues its commitment to parishioners centering on God's praise, becoming more like Jesus' disciples, building community and encouraging service and participation by all.

◆ St. Charles Borromeo Church

ST. JOSEPH ✦ PULASKI

✦ *Sketch of an earlier church*

The Indian Creek Township parish had mission churches on either side of the Tippecanoe River before a bridge was built. On the west side, a 16 x 24-foot St. Ann mission was built in 1852. In 1870 it was added to and used as a sacristy for a larger St. Francis of Assisi mission. On the river's east side, the Indian Creek settlement built a frame church in 1855, enlarged it in 1858, abandoned it in 1866, and after 1868 built Assumption of the Blessed Virgin Mary Church a mile and a half south of Pulaski. At an 1894 confirmation visit, Bishop Rademacher asked both churches to merge into St. Joseph Parish.

BISHOP JOSEPH RADEMACHER dedicated the brick Gothic St. Joseph Church at Pulaski on May 20, 1900. The church, which seats 300, has a 100-foot steeple. Having 106 households then, the parish has grown to about 140 households. This church was enlarged by a 30 x 62-foot apse in 1915. Later its stained-glass windows were installed. Precious Blood Missionaries have served this parish since 1873.

From 1852 priests from Logansport and Fort Wayne irregularly visited Pulaski County. From 1858 to 1862, Father Francis Nigh resided with a Pulaski family while caring for missions at Pulaski, Indian Creek, Winamac, Monterey, Turkey Creek, Klaasville, Crown Point, and Kewanna. Father Henry Koenig (1868-1872) from Winamac built a rectory at Indian Creek and arranged for a new church.

Precious Blood Missionary Father Willibald Siemers acquired one and a half acres opposite Pulaski on the river's east side. A rectory was completed in 1899. The parish has active organizations, finance and parish councils and a growing Order of Christian Initiation for Adults. For the church's centennial on July 15, 2001, Bishop William Higi celebrated a Mass of Thanksgiving, rededicating the redecorated edifice.

✦ *St. Joseph Church*

115

ST. JOSEPH ◆ REYNOLDS

◆ St. Joseph Church

◆ Interior of the church, 1951

THE present red brick and limestone, Romanesque style St. Joseph Church was built in summer 1876. The parish's 1866 mission church was moved and John Boon, Matthew Grissmer, Michael Vogel, James and Michael Britton, William Sala, Frank and Thomas Owens, and George Ruppert, among others, began building the 200-seating capacity edifice. Since Bishop Joseph Dwenger had put the Franciscan Friars in care of the mission from 1876-1888, Franciscan Father Dominic Meier oversaw St. Joseph's erection.

The Reynolds mission had been visited from Lafayette and Kentland since 1866. Earlier both Fathers George Hamilton and Joseph Stephan had been missionaries to its dozen Catholic families, including John and Bridget Horan and his brother William in 1854 and Michael and Elizabeth Vogel in 1856. Father Joseph Winter from St. Mary, Lafayette, directed the parishioners' building of the first St. Joseph Church on a land donation from Levi Reynolds. The $975 frame church seated 150 people. By 1907, the parish had 51 households of 282 persons.

St. Joseph's has seen several developments: a 1909 building addition, a cemetery purchased in 1912, the present rectory built in 1925, its 1945 Monticello

mission become a parish in 1952 and its parish hall expansion in 1954. In 1999, the parish renamed and dedicated the latter as Muller Hall. Since 2001, this hall and the rectory have been remodeled and interior and exterior church maintenance improvements were added, including three religious shrines behind the church.

The parish's 146 households of about 410 parishioners participate in active men's and women's organizations. In addition to promoting a full religious education program for its youth, it twins with St. John Neumann Church, Hode, Kentucky. St. Joseph's annual chicken or turkey October dinner has been an area attraction for more than 50 years.

◆ Sanctuary, 1976

◆ *St. Joseph Church*

ST. JOSEPH ◆ ROCHESTER

BISHOP JOHN NOLL dedicated brick Romanesque St. Joseph Church at 13th and Main streets on July 13, 1930. He appointed Father Charles Scholl Rochester's resident pastor in June 1941.

Rochester's first St. Joseph Church was on lots 446-447 at West 8th Street. From 1857 to 1858, Logansport priests regularly visited Rochester. On October 19, 1868, Bishop Luers purchased the lots for the church built in 1869. After 1871, priests from Wabash, Plymouth, Kokomo and Valparaiso attended until 1888. Called St. Paul's at the time priests from Valparaiso visited, St. Joseph's became Monterey's mission (1888-1941). In 1907, the parish had six households of 25 people.

With Lake Manitou's summer tourist growth in 1930, Monterey's pastor, Father John Schall, bought the present lots. After its last use on July 6, 1930, the frame church was razed and the present church built. Monterey's pastor cared for it until Father Scholl arrived to purchase a rectory. Father Harold Weller (1964-1978) built a new rectory with the parish hall. Father George Lanning (1957-1964) expanded the church and erected an outdoor shrine to Our Lady. In 1963 Father Lanning gave a historic lecture on "The Ecumenical Council of the Catholic Church" at a Protestant church. Father Richard Puetz, 1978-87, renovated the church interior in 1980 after adding the

church's south side handicapped ramp. Bishop Raymond Gallagher rededicated the church on October 19, 1980.

Father Francis Kilcline (1987-1994) reorganized the parish council after the diocesan structural pattern. In 1991, St. Ann, Kewanna, was assigned to Rochester's pastor. Father John Zahn (1994-2000) instituted the parish PT-715 radio program. With Father Joseph Jacob as pastor since 2000, St. Joseph's 250 households of about 850 parishioners are confident that the intercession of St. Joseph will continue bringing them growth and God's blessing.

◆ *Interior of the church*

117

ST. MARY ◆ DUNKIRK

◆ *The first church of St. Mary*

BISHOP RAYMOND GALLAGHER dedicated the present brick St. Mary Church on June 9, 1974. It contains the 1896 red brick, Gothic church's stained-glass windows. Hartford City's Father Charles Dhe oversaw its erection when Dunkirk's Catholic population had grown from 25 households to about 100 since 1863. Priests from Cincinnati and Union City said intermittent Masses in private homes. Father Dhe used the Todd Opera House until the church was built. In 1908, St. Mary's increased to 52 households of about 250 people.

In 1900, Dunkirk's first resident pastor, Father William Hogan, was also responsible for monthly Masses at St. Patrick, Redkey (1898-1949) and St. Anthony, Albany (1895-1902) that Father Dhe had also built. When the gas boom ended, population loss was reflected from 1922-1940 when St. Mary's and its missions were assigned to Portland. When another resident pastor, Father Joseph Lynn, was assigned to Dunkirk in 1941, a 1944 census revealed 45 Catholic households in all three towns. But during Father James Keane's pastorate (1961-1965), activity centered on the church's redecoration in 1964. By 1967, St. Mary's population grew to 119 households. Father Victor Schott (1965-1985) guided the building of the new St. Mary's church. At the dedication in 1974, the parish had 93 households of 281 people, increasing by 1996 to 106 households.

In 2002, St. Mary's received a lay parish coordinator, Mr. David Wilson, with Father Michael Ondo from Carmel as weekend sacramental minister. The parish population dipped to 52 households, but rose to 55 households of 142 by 2005 after clustering in 2004 with St. John the Evangelist, Hartford City, and St. Margaret, Montpelier.

◆ *St. Mary Church*

ST. JOHN THE EVANGELIST
◆ HARTFORD CITY

national Catholic weekly newspaper, Our Sunday Visitor. In 1922, the Ku Klux Klan peaked in Hartford City, driving some Catholic merchants out of business. After the 1929 Great Depression, Father Harold Moran's pastorate (1933-1961) provided a sense of stability. Father Edward Holland's (1961-1967) renovations fulfilled the Second Vatican Council's directives. Father Maurice Miller (1967-1972) introduced the pastoral council and budget committees. Father Leonard Reemmer (1972-1979) completely renovated the rectory. Father Leroy Kinnaman (1984-1991) again renovated the church and improved the grounds.

Through the 1980s, St. John's grew by many activities and an influx of Polish workers to a local factory. Among its several outreach apostolates, St. John has a sister parish in Haiti. Since 2004, St. John has been clustered with St. Margaret, Montpelier, and St. Mary, Dunkirk. Now a parish of 197 households, it has 406 parishioners.

◆ *St. John the Evangelist Church*

ON APRIL 24, 1898, Bishop Joseph Rademacher dedicated the brick, Gothic St. John the Evangelist Church seating 350. The parish had 300 households of 1,200 persons. Its growth from seven households in 1856 prompted the building of a frame church in 1883 for priests from Marion to serve twice a month. Hartford City's first resident pastor, Father Charles Dhe (1894-1906), also served missions at Poneto, Montpelier, Upland, Dunkirk, Redkey and Eaton.

In 1904, Holy Family School was built and run by Sisters of Providence and then Sisters of St. Francis Seraph of Perpetual Adoration until 1971, and in the 1980s, by Sisters of Notre Dame with lay teachers. A 1952 bequest from Mrs. A. F. Riedman replaced Holy Family School with St. John's Riedman Memorial School, which was dedicated on November 26, 1953. St. John's School closed in 2005.

The Parish Monthly pamphlet initiated by Father John Noll (1906-1910) in 1909 laid the foundation for the

The Parish Monthly

HARTFORD CITY, INDIANA, MARCH, 1910

JOHN F. NOLL, Pastor.

◆ *The Parish Monthly pamphlet*

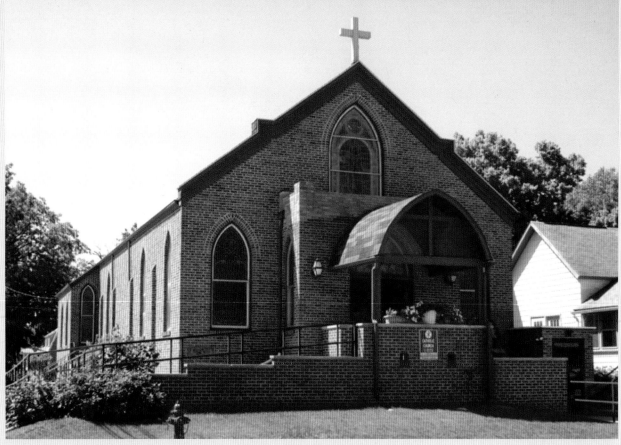

St. Margaret Church

ST. MARGARET ◆ MONTPELIER

BISHOP JOHN NOLL dedicated the present St. Margaret Church, Huntington Street, on June 10, 1941. It replaced two earlier St. John the Evangelist churches in Montpelier. The former churches were built in 1864 and 1896. The first, situated downtown, with seating capacity of 100, began with twelve households as a mission of Union City. Then from 1875, it was a mission of St. Lawrence, Muncie, for monthly services. The 1896 Gothic Revival church on Rockefeller Street had a commodious seven-room rectory. When the gas boom passed, the parish dwindled from 41 to 25 households.

Father Paul Welsh (1912-1914) had been Montpelier's only resident pastor. Montpelier returned to being a mission of Hartford City; then in 1920, of St. Joseph, Bluffton; in 1946-55, of Gas City; in 1955-58, of Marion; and from 1958 to 1959, of a DeMontfort Missionary. St. Margaret pastors were: Father James Quinn (1959-1961); Father Leonard Reemmer (1967-1972); Father Francis Niesen (1972-1980); Father William Holbrook (1980-1984); and Father Frederick Perry (1985-1997). Since 1997, it was administered in a cluster with St. John, Hartford City, and since 2004, also with St. Mary, Dunkirk.

About 85 percent of its 25 households today participate in some aspect of parish service living out the Mass. Among these are liturgical ministries, social concerns through a sister parish in Haiti, prison ministry and food pantry collections. There are also parish dinners for social and fund-raising purposes.

St. Margaret First Communion class, 1966

ST. FRANCIS OF ASSISI
◆ MUNCIE

◆ *St. Francis of Assisi Church*

◆ *Ceremonies of Blessing Mass, 1974*

Bishop William Higi dedicated the Ball State University Newman Center's new Florentine style worship space on November 20, 2003. Its Living Water mosaic baptismal font received the 2005 Bene Visual Arts Award in the Sacred Symbols and Architecture national competition sponsored by Resource Publications Ministry & Liturgy magazine. The new worship space expanded the worship facility at the Gallagher Multipurpose Center behind the Newman House on Riverside Avenue, which Bishop Raymond Gallagher dedicated on October 13, 1974.

On October 25, 1972, Bishop Gallagher had established the Newman Center as St. Francis of Assisi Parish and named St. Mary's parochial vicar, Father James Bates, its first pastor. The parish is for Ball State students and non-student family units associated with the university. The Newman Center developed from the 1966 Neely Avenue house where chaplains resided to meet with students nearer campus dormitories. Initially priests from St. Lawrence Church, especially Father Leo Pursley (1926-1930), did student ministry.

In 1930, Father Edgar Cyr of St. Mary's continued it when students Kathleen Meehan and Catherine Holden, alumna Margaret Ryan and faculty sponsor Ann Lautebauer chartered a Newman Club in 1939-1940. A 1956 Our Sunday Visitor Foundation grant built Noll Hall on Nichols to provide worship space for St. Mary's and a Newman Club office and lounge. The 1968 Neely house was purchased with the R. V. Achatz bequest, and staff expansion was provided by a grant from the Fort Wayne Friedman Foundation. In 1972, the Gallagher Multipurpose Center behind the Riverside Avenue Newman House was financed through the Diocese's Growth Fund and St. Mary's matching the Our Sunday Visitor's 1956 grant.

St. Francis Newman Center provides a wide variety of religious opportunities to the community, including four weekend Masses, daily liturgies, religious education classes and lectures on many contemporary subjects.

◆ *Dedication Mass, 2003*

IMMACULATE CONCEPTION ◆ PORTLAND

BISHOP JOHN CARBERRY dedicated the contemporary style, Bedford limestone Immaculate Conception Church on February 7, 1965. Its oak paneled interior with a terrazzo floor features laminated wood arches of wood plank and a black granite and limestone altar. Father Maurice Miller (1958-1967) oversaw its construction, replacing the 1876 frame structure that Precious Blood Father George Fleisch had erected for seven households.

Monthly Precious Blood Missionary visits from Mary's Home and Fort Recovery, Ohio, prior to 1873 prepared for the assignment of Father Joachim Baker as Portland's first resident pastor in 1888. Additions, extensions and alterations on both church and rectory marked parish growth. In 1907, the parish had 40 households of 180 persons.

Immaculate Conception School was built in 1958. After it closed in 1970, it provided religious education and parish meeting space. During Father Kenneth Raczek's pastorate (1967-1986), a church steeple was added and the Verdin Bell System and Carillon Chimes installed. In 1980, Father's mother, Ann Raczek, donated a Christ the King crucifix for the sanctuary. In 1971, Mrs. Gladys Hess had donated the church organ and in 1973, the generosity of Charles and Helen Barrenbrugge provided the church's air conditioning. By 1981, the parish had grown to 320 households of about 1,000 persons.

◆ *125th anniversary celebration, 2001*

Church and hall renovations continued during Father Joseph Grace's pastorate (1986-1998). The Immaculate Conception stained-glass window replaced the church front's original window. Since 1998, Father Martin Sandhage conducted further major improvements, especially the remodeling of the rectory.

Immaculate Conception has a full liturgical ministry and active parish organizations. Since 2001, the parish hosts a monthly Spanish Mass. It also supports six children through the Catholic Near East Welfare Association. Its growth today is at 345 households of about 1,270 persons.

◆ *Immaculate Conception Church*

ST. MARY ◆ UNION CITY

◆ *St. Mary Church*

◆ *Dedication of the church, 1892*

Bishop Joseph Rademacher dedicated the brick Gothic St. Mary Church seating 600 in 1892 for about 650 parishioners. It replaced Union City's second smaller brick church on Plum Street. The second church's bell was installed in the Gothic church.

Prior to 1865, missionaries from Cincinnati's Mount St. Mary of the West Seminary attended a log chapel built in 1856 on Joseph Weis' farm east of Union City, Ohio. Platted in 1849, Union City received its name from its location on the Indiana-Ohio border and reflected pre- and post-War Between the States patriotism. In addition, Union City became a hub for major railroads from 1852 to 1955. St. Mary's stately Victorian rectory was built in 1912 for numerous missionaries stopping between trains. Its garage features a double door to accommodate Model T Fords. In 2004, the rectory was renovated to its 1912 Craftsman architecture.

St. Mary School, 1877-1968, was endowed by Peter Kuntz to guarantee free Catholic education to any child attending it. On the razed school building's site, the present parish hall was built during Father John Zahn's pastorate (1985-1994).

Purchased in 1914, the church organ, flawed at installation, went unused until 1926. It was replaced in the 1970s with an electronic keyboard until restoration in 1991 by Wicks Organ Company. The parish discovered it has the first electrical-impulse organ in the world.

Presently 175 registered households participate in parish societies. At Father Alan Funk's advent in 1998, the church underwent a complete restoration. The parish holds the Miraculous Medal Novena, First Friday Sacred Heart devotions and Eucharistic Adoration, and since 2005, a monthly Mass in Spanish.

From 2003, St. Mary's pastor also administers St. Joseph, Winchester. The parish witnesses hope and promise for its members and the worldwide Church.

◆ *Church interior, 1950*

◆ *St. Joseph Church*

ST. JOSEPH ◆ WINCHESTER

BISHOP RAYMOND GALLAGHER dedicated the contemporary-style, brick St. Joseph Church on June 11, 1978. It replaced the frame structure that Father Jeremiah Quinlan from Union City had completed in 1882. The new church was erected on the 1875 property plus an addition purchased by Bishop John Carberry in 1962. Between 1889 and 1901, Father Michael Byrne frescoed the old church interior. In 1907, the parish had 10 households. St. Joseph's present cosmopolitan congregation likes to recall the Cummings,

Fitzmaurice, Doyle, Slusher, Lennon, Lafferty and McDonald pioneer families. It especially remembers Margaret (Cummings) Rhinehold and Frank Hickey.

In 1941, Union City's Winchester mission was assigned to Portland's pastor. Then in 1952, Bishop John Bennett purchased additional property and appointed Father John Cunningham Winchester's first resident pastor. The property's rectory was used until 1981 when Father Richard Smith bought a two-story house whose upstairs and basement were used for religious education classes until it was sold in 2005. During Father Louis Heitz's pastorate (1996-2003), classroom space for religious education was constructed in an area that joins the church and St. Joseph Hall. Bishop William Higi dedicated the Education Center on March 10, 2002, during the parish Golden Jubilee celebration.

St. Joseph Hall was completed in November 1965 and dedicated by Bishop Gallagher on June 12, 1966. During Father John Bouvier's tenure (1968-1972), plans for a new church unfolded. Groundbreaking took place on July 31, 1977, while Father George Askar oversaw the construction of the new, air-conditioned church dedicated the following June.

With complete religious education programs and a full parish staff and ministries, St. Joseph has outreach to Appalachia led by William and Mary Redmond. The ever-changing face that is St. Joseph today features 91 households of about 197 persons. Its pastor since 2003 is shared with St. Mary, Union City.

◆ *Golden Jubilee prayer card cover, 2002*